TEMPLATES
FOR MANAGING
TRAINING PROJECTS

Willis H. Thomas, PhD, PMP

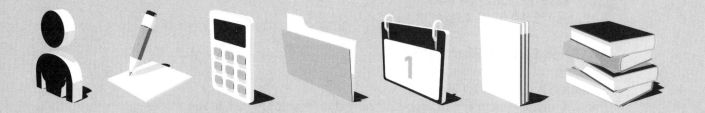

ATD Press is an internationally renowned source of insightful and practical information on workplace learning, training, and professional development.

ATD Press
1640 King Street
Alexandria, VA 22314

Ordering information: Books published by ATD Press can be purchased by visiting ATD's website at www.td.org/books or by calling 800.628.2783 or 703.683.8100.

Library of Congress Control Number: 2014945563
ISBN-10: 1-56286-917-5
ISBN-13: 978-1-56286-917-5
e-ISBN: 978-1-60728-431-4

ATD Press Editorial Staff:
Director: Glenn Saltzman
Manager: Ashley McDonald
Community of Practice Manager, Learning and Development: Juana Llorens
Associate Editor: Sarah Cough
Editorial Assistant: Ashley Slade
Cover Design: Bey Bello
Text Design: Lon Levy
Printed by Data Reproductions Corporation, Auburn Hills, MI.
www.datarepro.com

PMI® and PMBOK® are trademarks of Project Management Institute, Inc.

CONTENTS

INTRODUCTION

Are you a talent development professional who coordinates a variety of training projects? Do you experience challenges in maintaining documentation to meet your stakeholders' needs? Can your organization benefit from improved training forms to streamline processes? These are just a few examples in which training projects can benefit from well-designed forms. This is ATD's first book of project management templates and tools specifically designed for training professionals. It builds on the expertise of the two widely respected organizations: Project Management Institute (PMI®) and the Association for Talent Development (ATD). PMI® has created many resources for project managers, certifying hundreds of thousands of professionals worldwide. Similarly, ATD has set the standard for best practices in training and development through providing exemplary content and establishing a competency model for the talent development profession.

It may be helpful to consult a handbook or guide when using these templates. *A Guide to the Project Management Body of Knowledge* (PMBOK® Guide) presents industry-accepted project management terms, definitions, and guidelines. While the PMBOK® Guide is not required to use these templates, it can be very helpful for understanding the application of project management to your job function. It does this by organizing training activities through start-to-finish relationships (Process Groups) and logical categories (Knowledge Areas).

Templates for Managing Training Projects may also serve as a companion to other project management standards, such as PRINCE2 (Projects in Controlled Environments 2), and methodologies, such as Agile project management.

This book not only supports training project management, but also ongoing organizational and business functions, including human resource development functions such as, new hire orientation and professional development. Continually used forms are classified within the area of ongoing operations.

THE EMERGING ROLE OF THE TRAINING PROJECT MANAGER

The role of the training professional is increasingly changing and taking on a project management role that extends beyond training design and delivery into areas that support performance enhancement, process improvement, change management, quality assurance, and measurement and evaluation.

Training project management responsibilities can include authoring and maintaining the training project plan, including managing workflows; facilitating SME input; overseeing approvals; and ensuring effective management of the training project from start to finish. This often means:

- ensuring that competing demands (cost, time, scope, quality, risk, and resources) are properly addressed
- coordinating the efforts of the training project team (SMEs, instructional designers, curriculum developers, trainers, and training administrators)
- supporting training deliverables that have been produced for internal key stakeholders and external regulatory authorities.

The ATD Competency Model provides a framework that can benefit from the effective management of projects and related documentation. Projects are inherent in each area of the competency model—initiatives that are intended to address specific requirements. For example, in the area of change management, training projects might involve culture change and familiarization with new policies that name educating end-users as a primary task. Learning technologies might involve system validation to ensure compliance. Knowledge management might involve a variety of system implementations that require new ways of thinking, which necessitate learning and performance management as a core focus. Each of the components in the ATD Competency Model involves the development of products, services, or deliverables. In essence, this can be looked at as projects or sub-projects that are temporary, unique, and created for a specific purpose.

FIGURE 1: THE ATD COMPETENCY MODEL

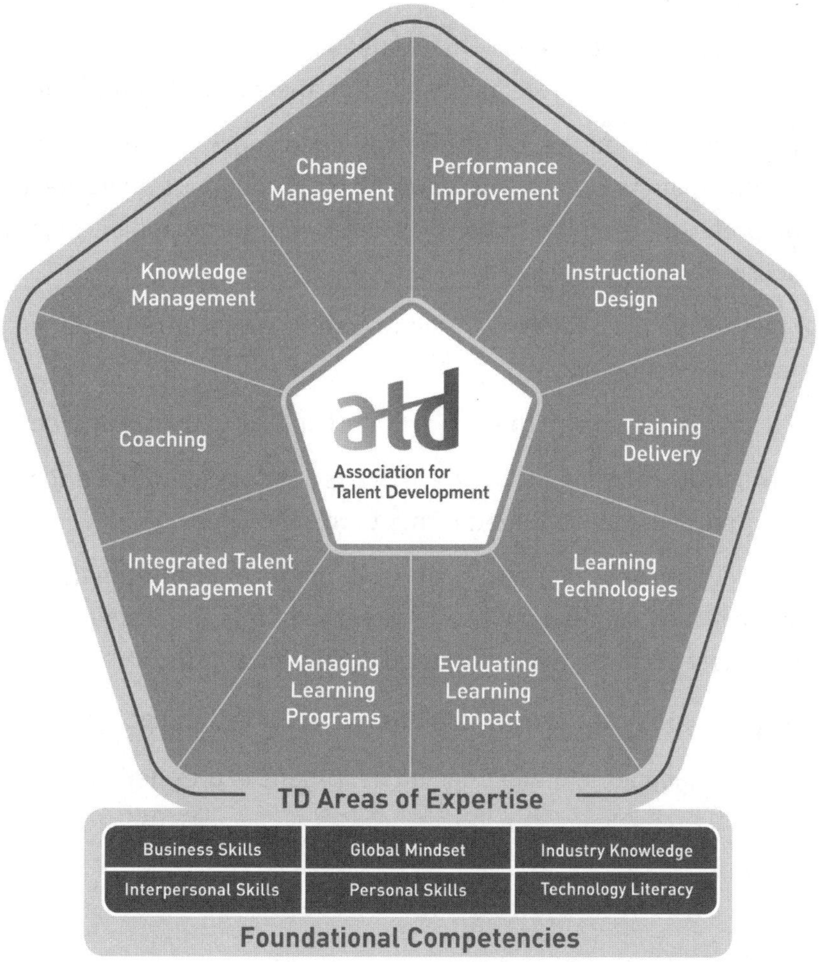

HOW TO USE THIS BOOK

This book is designed to be an invaluable resource to help manage learning and development projects. These forms are knowledge documents that have been conceptualized and enhanced with some input from contributors during the past 20-plus years. These customizable templates are practical for use on training-related projects or ongoing operations. "Training-related" refers to those initiatives that pertain to the full scope of training—from needs assessment to instructional design, from initiating a new training initiative to managing training operations.

To optimize the use of these forms consider the following:

- Why do you really need training forms? Do you need forms to track results, to show accountability, for formal documentation, or for other related concerns?

- Which forms do you need? Do you need all of the forms or just specific ones for particular projects based upon the size and complexity?

- When do you need the forms? Do you need specific forms at the beginning of the project and other forms throughout the project, or do you prefer utilizing the majority of the forms at the end of the project for record-keeping purposes?

- How will you use the forms? Will these be used as printed forms or electronic documents?

- Will they be used with the project team only or with stakeholders?

- Why do you need the form? Are there regulatory or compliance requirements that you need forms to track?

- Who will initiate, maintain, or approve the forms? Will the data administrator be responsible for the forms or is the training manager ultimately accountable for training documentation?

To make this book user friendly a glossary of terms that applies specifically to training project management and ongoing operations is provided at the end of this book. This will help you to develop a common language within your organization and ensure that everyone understands the concepts of training project management.

Whether you are a project manager who has responsibilities for training or a training and development professional who is responsible for managing training-related projects, you will find this guide useful.

The forms are organized by Knowledge Area (subsets of project management), according to the PMBOK® Guide, 5th edition:

1. **Project Communications Management** includes the ways in which we interact with people involved in the project and distribute information to them.

2. **Project Cost Management** includes the financial aspects of training projects, including the financial expenditures and budgets.

3. **Project Human Resource Management** includes onboarding and off-boarding of people involved in the project.

4. **Project Integration Management** is when all components of the project are brought into alignment through integrated change control, beginning with the business case and oversight.

5. **Project Procurement Management** includes deciding which external vendors will provide the solution for the training project.

6. **Project Quality Management** requires assurance that the project meets stakeholder expectations as outlined.

7. **Project Risk Management** addresses uncertainties and unknowns, and helps you come up with a plan of action to reduce their impact in the event they occur.

8. **Project Scope Management** maintains focus on the project so that the boundaries and parameters are in line with only the work that needs to be produced.

9. **Project Stakeholder Management** includes the identification and analysis of people involved in the project with respect to their level of power and interest in the training project.

10. **Project Time Management** is the duration it takes to complete a training project and the sequence of activities that needs to occur for it to be successful.

There are 47 project management processes identified in the PMBOK® Guide, grouped into 10 Knowledge Areas. According to PMI®, "A Knowledge Area represents a complete set of concepts, terms, and activities that make up a professional field, project management field, or area of specialization." It is recommended that you invest some time in becoming familiar with the PMBOK® Guide as the standard for project management. Browse it to see how the Knowledge Areas intersect with the Process Groups: Initiating, Planning, Executing, Monitoring/Controlling, and Closing.

Another popular reference for project management is PRINCE2, which is considered the second most popular project management standard in the world.

PRINCE2 focuses on seven principles:

1. continued business
2. learn from experience
3. defined roles and responsibilities
4. manage by stages
5. manage by exception
6. focus on products
7. tailor to suit the project environment.

There are also seven themes:

1. business case
2. organization
3. quality
4. plans
5. risk
6. change
7. progress.

While there are some inherent differences between these two project management standards, they are consistent in the guidelines and recommendations set forth in terms of how project management can be successfully carried out and the role of the project manager. The forms provided in this book can be adapted to work with both the PMBOK® Guide or PRINCE2. The PMBOK® Guide and PRINCE2 complement each other in the practical approaches that are recommended for project management.

In terms of those pursuing training and certification using these standards, PMI®, which publishes the PMBOK® Guide, has more than 500,000 people who have achieved certification, using the PMBOK® Guide as a foundation. This number is significantly higher than PRINCE2. For this reason and others, this book of forms follows the PMBOK® Guide as an easy to adapt to framework.

For those training professionals who will reference the PMBOK® Guide, you should pay particular attention to how each Knowledge Area coincides with each Process Group. This can be thought of in general terms as the competing demands you will experience when dealing with training projects. Examples include time (schedule), risk (unknowns), and cost (budget). The training forms included in this book can help you to document and develop strategies to address these issues.

SPECIAL CONSIDERATIONS WHEN USING THIS BOOK

Keep in mind that while there are many forms in this book, streamlined documentation is nearly always appreciated. However, regulatory or compliance requirements may necessitate robust documentation. In this case, these forms can support seamless administration within a project management office (PMO). The purpose of a PMO is to maintain forms to simplify and standardize project management. At the end of the day, it is all about improving documentation and related processes throughout your organization.

Sometimes change is not easy. To acclimate your colleagues to the idea of better project documentation, consider holding an orientation meeting to discuss the benefits of standardizing forms and using the same templates. Many will embrace the idea, while others may need convincing about the advantages. They may be initially resistant and prefer to continue doing things their own way. It is important to help these individuals consider the many benefits of standardization. Some organizations may find it preferable to do it a little at a time, while others may find it better to implement the new forms all at once. The benefit of implementing all the forms at once is that it can provide a fresh start for the new and improved method of managing training documentation. The advantage of doing it over time is that it helps people adapt to the new system more slowly and can ease the change management process. Whatever path you decide to take, it is important to get buy-in from key stakeholders.

As you use this book to improve and maintain your training documentation, it is important to avoid:

- Slowing down current processes that will not benefit from additional training related forms.
- Over-customizing forms so that they lose all original context. In this case, it may be better to create a new form entirely with another name.
- Being too rigid; the forms are templates and may need a little customization to fit your exact needs.

Consider a real world example. Your team is working on a new project. You load all of the forms onto a server with little instruction because you are a very busy training manager. People may begin using the forms and find them useful, but some could be customized without your approval. To control modifications of the forms, develop a job aid that addresses training documentation and the appropriate use of the forms. Keep track of the forms that are being modified and help with revisions when practical. It is important to keep in mind the problems that can occur if there is no oversight of the training documentation. Even with excellent resources, poor overall management can result in out-of-date forms and poor record keeping. The solution to this issue is to ensure that someone is accountable for training documentation.

TARGET AUDIENCE

Templates for Managing Training Projects is written for those who have roles and responsibilities in training and development and those who manage training projects. This includes a wide variety of job titles and functional areas, such as:

- learning and development professionals who are typically responsible for the maintenance of training forms
- project management professionals who may utilize the forms for tracking training deliverables
- quality operations staff who may use the forms for conducting training audits
- human resources staff who can use the forms for tracking performance improvement
- procurement professionals who may use the forms to keep up-to-date on vendor communications as it relates to the creation of training programs
- legal departments that may express interest in training documentation to ensure training compliance.

In addition to those who use the forms, there are many people who have supporting roles who will receive these forms, such as curriculum developers, instructional designers, training data entry, and administration. Almost anyone, and sometimes everyone, may become involved in training and development initiatives as a facilitator or recipient. Training touches every department and function and can be situated cross-functionally within the organization. In addition consultants or those who have small training functions can benefit from the use of these training forms.

TRAINING PROJECTS VERSUS ONGOING OPERATIONS

There is some disagreement as to what differentiates a training project from an ongoing training operation. In this book, training projects have a beginning and an end, are unique, and serve a specific purpose to produce a product, service, or result. A product could include an instructor guide, a service could include an instructor-led training session, and a result could be the test scores of participants who took the training. Ongoing operations are tasks that emerge from training projects; are the result of a training project, are in some way connected to a training project; or are continuous, repeated, or identical. Ongoing operations may include the delivery of the same training program to different audiences.

Some organizations initiate a training project that transitions to an ongoing operation. For example, the training project could be developing a training program to assist customer service representatives with using the new customer relations management (CRM) system, while an ongoing operation could be updating the CRM training to reflect system changes. They will then submit a request to enhance this ongoing training operation, but refer to it as a project. It is not the purpose of this book to debate the iterative nature of project management or the complex relationships that exist between project management and ongoing operations. Rather it is the intent to improve the organization, management, and documentation for training in both training project management and ongoing operations. These forms are cross-functional and can be used for training projects or ongoing operations; for example, by allowing the learning and development professional to coordinate training functions through the use of the forms.

IT'S TRAINING IN THE PUREST SENSE OF THE WORD

Some people are sensitive to the use of the word training (in part due to its perceived overuse as a category). As a result, they shy away from referring to themselves as conducting training or being trainers. They may use other terms to describe their function (learning and development, organization development, or facilitation). We could agree perhaps that training is what we perform and learning is what people do. That said, we will use "training" and "training-related" as the overarching terms to refer to training project management and ongoing operations. This can include:

- needs assessment
- instructional design
- curriculum development
- learning management system implementation
- media creation
- training measurement/metrics
- instructor-led training
- policy and procedure development.

A WIDER VIEW OF PROJECT AND IMPROVEMENT CYCLES

There are a variety of project and improvement cycles that include training. It is important to understand these approaches when using the forms. This section takes an integrated view of training using various methodologies and approaches. These are for illustration purposes only and it is not a linear relationship. As most trainers know, during the initiating or analysis phase you're also planning your schedule, costs, quality measurement, risk analysis, communication strategy, measurement, closing, and so on, as you define your scope. So while the forms are categorized into Knowledge Areas, there may be some instances in which the forms need to be reclassified to fit specific categories. For example, you may find that combining the Cost and Procurement Knowledge Areas into a single category called Expenditures is more desirable. Tailor the forms to your specific require-ments to improve their utility.

FIGURE 2: EVOLUTION FROM QUALITY MANAGEMENT TO ISD

DEMING QUALITY CYCLE	PROJECT MANAGEMENT	ISD
Plan	Initiate	Analysis
Do	Plan	Design
Check	Execute	Development
Act	Monitor	Implementation
Monitor	Close	Evaluation

The Project Management Connection to Instructional Systems Design and Quality Improvement

Can instructional systems design (ISD) benefit from the experiences and the best practices found with project management templates? Furthermore, what about the lessons learned within the quality movement? The first transition is an easy one, because, at one level, the traditional ISD model is in fact a project management model. In addition, it captures and codifies a number of best practices from everyday experiences.

For example, the classic ISD model that was created in the 1970s for the Training and Doctrine Command of the U.S. military can be traced back to the best training practices that evolved from the various Job Corps projects in the 1960s. The answer to the second question, the importance of the TQM movement in shaping and influencing the classic ISD model, is similar because they all share the same parent-child relationship. The modern quality movement can be directly traced back to the 1950s with Deming's plan, do, check, act cycle; the continuous cycle was repeated again and again with a monitoring function until a defect-free product or service emerged.

Adapted from the *ASTD Handbook for Workplace Learning Professionals*.

From the perspective of the PMBOK® Guide, projects are viewed from the perspective of Process Groups:

- Initiating: Determine the project type and scope.
- Planning: Plan the amount of time, cost, and resources required to adequately estimate the work.
- Executing: Begin the work of the project, including management of resources.

- Monitoring and Controlling: Manage oversight, continuous improvement, and lessons learned.
- Closing: Complete formal acceptance of the project, archiving documentation, and final evaluation.

Some organizations have adopted a Lean Six Sigma environment and as a result they may adhere to DMAIC principles. During the Monitoring and Controlling phase of a project, there may be some concern for quality and DMAIC may be engaged. This is a process improvement methodology that is commonly (but not exclusively) associated with Six Sigma.

- Define: Outline the business issues, objectives, resources, scope, and timeline. This information is captured in the project charter.
- Measure: Set current levels as the basis for improvement by collecting data.
- Analyze: Verify and choose a root cause for elimination.
- Improve: Determine, test, and implement a solution to address the issue.
- Control: Focus on the sustainability of the solution.

During the Improve phase of DMAIC, a training intervention, such as a job-aid or e-learning module may be defined. This will require instructional design and thus we might look at using ADDIE:

- Analysis: Explore training and development objectives and determine gaps.
- Design: Define the learning objectives, content, delivery method, and assessments.
- Develop: Create the content (storyboards, slides, graphics, participant guides, e-learning, and so on).
- Implement: Pilot and roll out the training.
- Evaluate: Measure the effectiveness and efficiency of the training deliverables.

Considering that evaluation is an iterative process, in the final stage of ADDIE, we may consider Kirkpatrick's Four Levels of Evaluation:

1. Reaction: Did they like the training?
2. Knowledge check: Did they learn from the training?
3. Behavior change: Were there changes in performance?
4. Results: Did training have an effect?

If the focus is on Level 4 Results, then we may address the impact to the organization. Quite often, we look to measure training effectiveness or efficiency with respect to resource utilization. There are seven categories of resources in this book: people, money, systems, facilities, equipment, materials, and supplies.

MANAGING AND ORGANIZING YOUR DOCUMENTATION

Maintaining training forms is much easier if it is an organized process. There are two ways to maintain training forms—electronic and paper-based. Electronic systems can use completed and saved documents, completed forms converted to PDF, forms in either format saved in a database, multi-user collaboration on the intranet or cloud, or scanned copies of forms that have been filled out by hand. Paper-based systems are generally hard copies of completed documents in a filing system.

The design of this book provides an option for both electronic and paper-based methods. The forms included in this book can be photocopied and filled out from the physical book or downloaded as PDF forms from the book's website at td.org/books. Organizations should begin by defining a folder structure for the documents that will be created. This will be different if physical filing cabinets are used instead of shared file folders on computer hard drives (or servers). Be sure to adhere to good business practices and good documentation procedures regarding records management, especially if there are compliance or regulatory requirements for document archiving and retrieval.

Where practical, here are some helpful suggestions you may want to consider when organizing training forms:

- Create a main folder; for example, Training Project Management Forms.
- Create sub-folders within each folder; for example, one for each category, including Project Communications Management.
- Within each subfolder create a timeline folder; for example, january_2014.
- Avoid leaving spaces in folder names, because this can sometimes cause hyperlinks to break. Instead use underscores to separate logical attributes of labels. For example, January_2014.
- Use caution when defining labels. Some servers look at the same spelling as three different words; for example, January, january, and JANUARY are not the same.
- Be careful with special (unique) characters. People who use tablets and smartphones may have a limited keyboard that does not display special characters.
- Keep the length of labels to a reasonable number of characters.
- Avoid uncommon abbreviations, which may not be understood by the users accessing the files.
- If using numbers and letters, use intuitive patterns.
- Alphabetize folders or numerically sequence.
- Minimize the number of subfolders to reduce extensive drilling down to access the desired file.
- Consider putting an index with instructions in main or subfolders that helps describe contents of files within that folder.
- Files within folders should have a creation/revision dates.
- Any files that use encryption for security reasons should be noted; for example, Training_Form_(Secure).

- If files are opened and re-saved, but not modified, they will have a different system date. Users should be informed that the system date and revision date are two different things.

- Change the revision date when you make any revisions to a TPM form.

- A revision history should be available on the form itself or in an indexed file in the same folder or subfolder for tracking purposes.

THE TRAINING PROJECT PLAN

A training project plan typically consists of a series of related plan documents that describe how each phase of the training project will be managed. It may include how communications will be handled, budgets controlled, risks addressed, and time accounted for in terms of resource utilization. There is no pre-defined length to a training plan. It will vary depending upon the circumstances.

A training project plan is unnecessary when:

- The training-related tasks are short, simple, and informal.
- There is no perceived value to having a training project plan.

A training project plan is beneficial when:

- Training is a formal process.
- Dynamically changing educational needs exist; for example, the use of Agile project management methodologies for software development requires training programmers on business processes.
- Regulatory compliance, and audits of the training system and records have identified gaps that now require formal procedures to train employees.
- There are complex systems—for example, SAP, Oracle, PeopleSoft ERP systems—that require detailed storyboarding.
- Vendor-managed programs and outsourced training and development programs necessitate longer development cycles.
- The project includes collaborative initiatives to develop programs that benefit multiple organizations for the purpose of training groups of people, such as certification programs.

FIGURE 3: TRAINING PROJECT PROCESS MAP

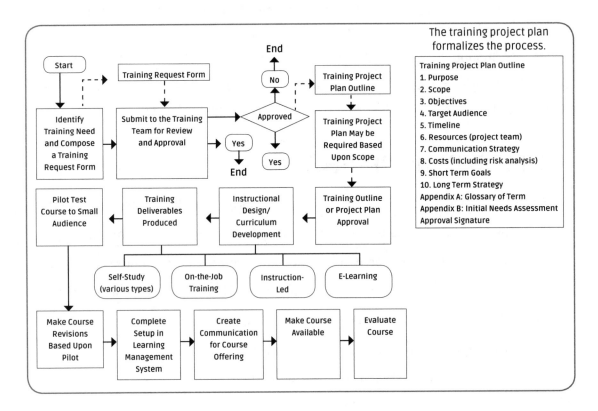

Figure 3 above represents the detailed steps that may be required in a large-scale or complex training project plan. Simpler versions of a training project plan may include only a training request, which is followed by training approvals (from management) and creation of deliverables; for instance, instructor-led training.

Training project plans should take into special consideration:

- Cost: Training-related expenditures, including LMS implementation and travel costs. It may also be appropriate to include costs associated with risks.

- Quality: The degree to which the project fulfills requirements determines quality. For example, a job aid may work well for training people on the manufacturing floor for just-in-time information needs, but might not be suitable for addressing long, step-by-step procedures.

- Resources: Include people, budgets, facilities, systems, equipment, materials, and supplies required on a dedicated, temporary, and pooled resource basis.

- Risk: Training is impacted by risk when some aspects are uncertain. Those involved in risk management identify and plan options in order to reduce or eliminate the potential risk. An example might include a key resource accepting a different position at another company.

- Scope: Define of the target audience and parameters of the project.

- Stakeholders: Internal or external people impacted by the training deliverable either using it or supporting it.

- Time: To measure time create duration estimates for training-related activities.

GETTING STARTED

By this point, you may be anxious to use the forms. The following is some quick start information:

- If you are currently using training forms, compare your existing forms to those in the book.

- Some of these forms are situation-specific. For example, there are some forms that are focused on training compliance and the most appropriate use of these forms may be during an internal audit.

- The forms may be used in hard copy or electronic format.

- Some of the forms have been pre-populated with examples to suggest ways in which these fields may be completed.

The sections align with the PMBOK® Guide and begin with the project plan for each knowledge area. The forms contained within the knowledge areas are listed in the plan document under the following headings.

1. Training Communications Management: Who gets what information, in what form, and when?

2. Training Cost Management: What are the expenditures, how are they paid for, and who is paying for them?

3. Training Human Resource Management Plan: How are people acquired and released from the project?

4. Training Integration Management: How is the project viewed holistically to ensure all the required work is being performed?

5. Training Procurement Management: How are make versus buy decisions made and what is the process to source for external resources?

6. Training Quality Management: How do we know that the product of the project is meeting stakeholder expectations?

7. Training Risk Management: What solutions are put in place to avoid, accept, transfer, or mitigate unknown circumstances that could potentially affect the project?

8. Training Scope Management: What metrics can be put in place to ensure that only the work required is performed and that additional requests are appropriately monitored through approval processes, such as change controls?

9. Training Stakeholder Management: When aligning with those who have a vested interest in the project, what can be done to ensure good working relationships?

10. Training Time Management: How do we determine the timeframes, establish milestones, and determine durations for project tasks?

As you look to add, delete, or revise forms, please consider using this framework to support training documentation.

MULTI-USER INPUT TO FORMS

An emerging and popular use of training forms is to have multiple users view and provide input into the form simultaneously. This can be done in a number of ways using screen-sharing software or holding a web-based conference. There are cost-effective options (or in some cases free of charge) multi-user platforms with real time updates that embrace collaboration—Google Drive (free or paid) and MS Office 365 (paid) are two. Alternative screen sharing options include Skype and Google Hangouts (free and paid). Whatever you decide, it is important to realize that technology is continually changing. Use these ground rules to help the project go more smoothly:

- Set aside an adequate amount of time to design the form.
- Ensure the person who will be entering the information into the form has great listening skills.
- Make changes now to reduce the number of revisions that have to be made at a later time.
- Minimize the use of complex graphics and illustrations.
- Standardize the form so it has a consistent look and feel.

MANAGING COMMUNICATIONS

Managing communications involves planning, collecting, creating, distributing, storing, retrieving, managing, controlling, monitoring, and distributing project information.

Those involved in training projects and ongoing operations have many ways to communicate:

- phone (office, home, and mobile)
- email
- text message
- instant message
- web conference
- video conference
- face-to-face
- social media
- formal reports and presentations.

Communication methods are an integral part of training delivery methods and it is essential for training professionals to be masters of communication. Training is delivered in many ways, but sometimes the method of documentation is different. It needs to be standardized for the following methods of training:

- instructor-led

- self-study

- group study

- e-learning

- computer-based training

- on-the-job training

- role play

- simulation

- mobile learning.

Therefore, a significant focus should be placed on communication within the project team and to stakeholders. This is especially important during training delivery. Training forms can help document many things, including:

- verbal communication

- non-verbal communication (body language)

- tone (para-linguistics)

- foreign language, speech interpretation, and pronunciation

- cultural awareness

- virtual workplaces

- meeting facilitation

- presentation skills

- influencing

- negotiation

- conflict resolution.

Forms help communications processes in many ways, including:

- ensuring that people know when, where, and how training will be delivered

- selecting the methods of training to support blended-learning solutions

- helping facilitators remain cognizant of both verbal and non-verbal communication.

The PMBOK® Guide says Project Communications Management includes the processes required to ensure timely and appropriate planning, collection, creation, distribution, storage, retrieval, management, control, monitoring, and the ultimate dissemination of project information.

To manage project communications you must:

- Plan communications management.
- Manage communications.
- Control communications.

The communication forms in this section include:

1. Training Communications Management Plan
2. Training Announcement
3. Training Body Language and Tone Checklist
4. Training Communication Solution Matrix
5. Training Kickoff Meeting Agenda
6. Training Lessons Learned
7. Training Logistics Checklist
8. Training Meeting Agenda
9. Training Meeting Minutes
10. Training Status Report

Training Communications Management Plan

Project Title: _____

Project Description:

Planning communications management will involve:

Managing communications will involve:

Controlling communications will involve:

Notes:

Prepared by: _____ Date: _____

Contact Information: _____

Project Manager: _____ Project Due Date: _____

Training Announcement

Course Title: _____

Course Description: _____

Course Objectives: _____

Target Audience: _____

Course Location: _____

Directions to the Course Location: _____

_____

Course Start Time:_____ Course End Time: _____

Prerequisites: _____

Primary Contact for Course: _____

Email: _____

Phone:_____

Facilitator/Trainer for the Course:_____

Course Provided by ☐ Internal Resource ☐ Vendor _____

Course Fees:_____

Registration Deadline: _____

Number of Seats Available: _____

To Register for the Course, Go to: _____

To Register for the Course, Contact: _____

Alternate Dates for the Course: _____

For Hotel and Travel Accommodations, Contact: _____

Notes:

Prepared by: _____ Date: _____

Contact Information: _____

Project Manager: _____ Project Due Date: _____

Training Body Language and Tone Checklist

Project Title: _____

Project Description:

The following are body language (non-verbal communication) clusters. What did you see exhibited?

- Attentive: seems to show real interest and concern

- Bored: lacking concern

- Closed: distrusting or reserved

- Deceptive: lying, covering up, or hiding

- Emotional: seeking to gain empathy

- Friendly: warm and welcoming, usually accompanied by physical touch

- Greeting: formal, professional, intent on making a good impression

- Hurried: in a rush

- Intimidating: appearing to show power, may be threatening

- Jumping: excited, celebrating

- Kidding: not meant to be taken seriously, joking

- Lazy: unresponsive, tired

- Military: a postured stance indicating available for duty

- Nurturing: caressing, loving, and embracing

- Open: trying to be transparent

- Partaking: engaging, sharing, and experiencing

- Quiet: silent, subdued

- Romantic: inferring physical desire or attraction to someone else

- Submissive: indicating ready to give in

- Testing: questioning, asking, inquiring

- Understanding: reasoning

- Vindictive: attack mode

- Watching: surveying or observing

- X-Ray: attempting to look through to gain more insight

- Yearning: strong desire

- Zone: keeping a distance or setting parameters

Non-Verbal Communication (Body Language)

Person	Action/Gesture	What It Suggests

Tone of Voice (Paralinguistics)

Person	Tone	What It Suggests

Person	Mood, Attitude, or Behavior	What It Suggests

Diction: Words and terms they use (formal, casual, or slang) _____

Notes:

Prepared by: _____ Date: _____

Contact Information: _____

Project Manager: _____ Project Due Date: _____

Training Communication Solution Matrix

Project Title: _____

Project Description:

Date: _____

Meeting Topic: _____

Number of Attendees: _____

Name	One-on-One (Face-to-Face) Meeting	Group (Face-to-Face) Meeting	Audio Teleconference (Call-in)	Webinar With Slides and Voice (Virtual)	Webinar With Webcam, Slides, and Voice	Other

Notes:

Prepared by: _____   Date: _____

Contact Information: _____

Project Manager: _____   Project Due Date: _____

Training Kickoff Meeting Agenda

Project Title: _____

Project Description:

Sponsor Remarks:

Project Team Introductions:

Presentation of the Training Project Plan and Highlights:

Question and Answers From Participants:

Notes:

Prepared by: _____ Date: _____

Contact Information: _____

Project Manager: _____ Project Due Date: _____

Training Lessons Learned

Project Title: _____

Project Description:

Key Learning (Summative)

Issue	Done Right (R)	Done Wrong (W)	Done Differently (D)	Impact, Results, Accountability

Issue	Done Right (R), Done Wrong (W), or Done Differently (D)	Assigned to	Process Improvement Action

Notes:

Prepared by: _____ Date: _____

Contact Information: _____

Project Manager: _____ Project Due Date: _____

Training Logistics Checklist

Project Title: _____

Project Description:

Facilities

☐ Confirm the location of reserved room.

☐ Publish street address and crossroads to easily locate using GPS.

☐ Confirm room will be available 30 minutes before start.

☐ Confirm facilities contacts for the room.

☐ Confirm signs have been posted to direct people to the room.

☐ Check environment for appropriate air temperature (heating/cooling).

☐ Obtain portable heaters if the room is cold.

☐ Obtain fans if necessary.

☐ Check ventilation in the room.

☐ Check lighting/brightness.

☐ Check environment for garbage, leave behinds, personal items of others, and handle as appropriate.

☐ Check environment for smells, odors, and fragrances, and be prepared with an air freshener if necessary.

☐ Check environment for cleanliness.

☐ Check accommodations for handicapped people.

☐ Check availability of additional chairs and tables.

☐ Place additional chairs at the back of the room.

☐ Other: _____

Equipment

☐ Check for the availability to have a projector in the room.

☐ Test quality of the projector in the room.

☐ Check microphones.

☐ Check the connection from the laptop to the projector.

☐ Check speakers in the room.

☐ Set music volume.

☐ Check prerecorded music in the room.

☐ Check if a whiteboard or smartboard is available.

☐ Check if a photocopier is available.

☐ Check if an easel is available.

☐ Check if a printer is available.

☐ Other: _____

Safety, Security, and Wellness

☐ Safety and emergency issues reviewed.

☐ Notify site security of visitors.

☐ Ensure that any external visitors have parking passes.

☐ Facilities reviewed for, the location of restrooms and exits.

☐ Emergency procedures covered.

☐ Other: _____

Communications

☐ Ensure an announcement about the training has been sent out two to four weeks prior to the event.

☐ Ensure a follow-up announcement about the training has been sent out one week prior to the event.

☐ Ensure a welcome announcement about the training has been sent out one day prior to the event.

☐ Prepare roster for trainer/facilitator.

☐ Create a sign-in sheet.

☐ Have participants introduce themselves.

☐ Conduct an appropriate icebreaker activity.

☐ Verify everyone has signed the sign-in sheet.

☐ Create a thank-you letter for participants attending session.

☐ Other: _____

Refreshments

☐ Contact caterer one month before the event.

☐ Confirm delivery of refreshments one day before the event.

☐ Confirm breakfast refreshments.

☐ Confirm lunch refreshments.

☐ Confirm dinner refreshments.

☐ Confirm number of cups.

☐ Confirm water.

☐ Confirm coffee.

☐ Other: _____

Materials and Supplies

☐ Print name tents.

☐ Print name tags.

☐ Print names on certificates of participation.

☐ Print necessary handouts (consider providing electronic copies through email or download link).

☐ Check availability of supplies:

- whiteboard markers and eraser

- copier paper

- easel paper

- pens

- notepaper

- pencils
- sticky notes
- boxes of tissues
- tape
- scissors
- staplers
- other: _____

Assessments

- Distribute Level 1 assessment (satisfaction survey) after course delivery.
- Collect Level 1 assessment after course delivery.
- Distribute Level 2 assessment (knowledge check, quiz, test, or other) after course delivery.
- Collect Level 2 assessment after course delivery.
- Other: _____

Notes:

Prepared by: _____ Date: _____

Contact Information: _____

Project Manager: _____ Project Due Date: _____

Training Meeting Agenda

Project Title: _____

Project Description:

Discussion Topics:

Highlights From Previous Meeting Minutes:

Agenda

8:30–9:00 Refreshments and Welcome

9:00–9:30 Overview of New Training Program

9:30–10:00 Demonstration of New Software

10:00–10:15 Morning Break

10:15–10:30 Review of Job Aids

10:30–10:45 Review of Instructor-Led Training

10:45–11:15 Review of Procedure

11:15–11:45 LMS Administration

11:45–12:30 Lunch

12:30–2:15 Train-the-Trainer Best Practices

2:15–2:30 Afternoon Break

2:30–4:30 Open Lab to Support End-User Testing

Notes:

Prepared by: _____ Date: _____

Contact Information: _____

Project Manager: _____ Project Due Date: _____

Training Meeting Minutes

Project Title: _____

Project Description:

Scheduled Meeting

Date	
Time	
Location	
Facilitator	
Minutes Prepared by	
In Attendance Locally	
In Attendance Virtually	
Other	

Discussion Topic	Highlights	New Action Item

Previous Action Item	Completed by	Details

Notes:

Prepared by: _____ Date: _____

Contact Information: _____

Project Manager: _____ Project Due Date: _____

Training Status Report

Project Title: _____

Project Description:

Milestones Achieved or Missed:

Status of Deliverables:

Critical Success Factors (CSFs):

Key Performance Indicators (KPIs):

Earned Value Analysis:

Other Measurement Methods to Show Project Performance:

Notes:

Prepared by: _____ Date: _____

Contact Information: _____

Project Manager: _____ Project Due Date: _____

MANAGING COST

Managing cost involves planning, estimating, budgeting, financing, and controlling project costs to ensure they stay within the allocated budget.

People involved in training projects and ongoing operations must be mindful of how they manage finances because training is commonly viewed as a cost to the organization. While training may be highly valued, the training budget is often reduced when the financial outlook is bleak. It is important to justify the investment in training, showing both tangible and intangible benefits; for example, lowered training costs and increased employee morale. Mandatory training is usually easier to justify. Websites that provide training heuristics are an essential part of estimating the cost of training projects. Use these references to determine how long it should take to develop training content, including instructor-led training materials, e-learning courses, and similar. One example is www.chapmanalliance.com/howlong. You can also benchmark training costs by reviewing training and development trade journals or training and development professional association websites, such as ATD.

Training budgets are often decentralized, so each department may have different amounts of money set aside for professional development, performance improvement, certification, and employee motivation and team-building. Training budgets are frequently based upon historical spending, unless there are new initiatives with detailed costs presented. The cost of quality relates to the value of the training in terms of preventing errors, which can result in rework or returns. Defend good training programs by linking them to quality.

Estimating techniques need to be simplified for those involved in training:

- Training programs use an individual unit pricing approach (also known as bottom-up estimating) to determine individual components, such as the manuals required and facilities needed.

- Historical pricing (also known as analogous estimating methods) is also beneficial for training when comparing previous expenditures to current costs or previous expenditures to planned future expenditures; for example, large conferences.

- Cost control is effectively handled using spreadsheets and simple visuals that compare line item costs, such as pie charts and bar charts.

Forms help in the area of cost in many ways, including:

- allocating training budgets to avoid cost overruns

- determining whether it is more cost effective to deliver training internally or hiring a vendor

- tracking the level of effort that it takes to create a training program.

The PMBOK® Guide says Project Cost Management includes the processes involved in planning, estimating, budgeting, financing, funding, managing, and controlling costs so the project can be completed within the approved budget.

To manage cost you must:

- Plan cost management.

- Estimate costs.

- Determine budget.

- Control costs.

The cost forms in this section include:

1. Training Cost Management Plan

2. Training Budget Cost Estimator Worksheet

3. Training Cost-Benefit Analysis

4. Training Heuristics Rule of Thumb

5. Training Make or Buy Determination

Training Cost Management Plan

Project Title: _____

Project Description:

Planning cost management will involve:

Estimating cost will involve:

Determining budget will involve:

Controlling costs will involve:

Notes:

Prepared by: _____ Date: _____

Contact Information: _____

Project Manager: _____ Project Due Date: _____

Training Budget Cost Estimator Worksheet

Project Title: _____

Project Description:

Actual Expenditures

Date	Training Deliverable	Initial Cost	Ongoing Cost	Internally Created (Y/N)	Externally Acquired (Y/N)

Quarter	Cost	Cost Center	Training Deliverable(s)
1st Quarter			
1st Quarter			
2nd Quarter			
2nd Quarter			
3rd Quarter			
3rd Quarter			
4th Quarter			
4th Quarter			
Totals			
Total Training Budget:			

Notes:

Prepared by: _____ Date: _____

Contact Information: _____

Project Manager: _____ Project Due Date: _____

Training Cost-Benefit Analysis

Project Title: _____

Project Description:

Deliverable Itemization

Date	Training Deliverable	Initial Cost	Ongoing Cost	Short-Term Benefit	Long-Term Benefit

Factors associated with initial cost:

Factors associated with ongoing cost:

Notes:

Prepared by: _____ Date: _____

Contact Information: _____

Project Manager: _____ Project Due Date: _____

Training Heuristics Rule of Thumb

Project Title: _____

Project Description:

Level of Effort

Training Deliverable	Time to Create	Number of Resources	Skill Set (who) Internal/ External	Special Considerations	Monetary Value
Audio Narration Scripting					
Audio Narration Recording					
Needs Assessment					
Instructor Guide					
Participant Guide					
Paper Job Aid					
PowerPoint Presentation					
Level 1 Evaluation					

Training Deliverable	Time to Create	Number of Resources	Skill Set (who) Internal/ External	Special Considerations	Monetary Value
Level 2 Evaluation					
Level 3 Evaluation					
Level 4 Evaluation					
ROI Analysis					

Notes:

Prepared by: _____ Date: _____

Contact Information: _____

Project Manager: _____ Project Due Date: _____

Training Make or Buy Determination

Project Title: _____

Project Description:

Develop or Acquire

Date	Training Deliverable	Make					Buy Estimated Vendor Cost
		Number of Resources and Type	Total People Hours To Develop	Estimated Resource Expense Converted	One -Time Costs (Software/ Hardware)	Total Estimated Make Expense	

Other factors that should be considered to support make or buy decision:

Notes:

Prepared by: _____ Date: _____

Contact Information: _____

Project Manager: _____ Project Due Date: _____

MANAGING HUMAN RESOURCES

Managing human resources involves coordinating and overseeing project team members. This includes management and leadership.

The training team is frequently a part of the human resources department and as a result may be directly and indirectly involved with developing people by conducting:

- new hire and transfer orientation
- professional development
- performance evaluation
- on-the-job training
- coaching and mentoring.

Supporting the human resource effort includes multiple audiences:

- part-time and full-time employees
- external clients
- external contractors, including suppliers, consultants, and vendors.

Forms support human resources processes in many ways, such as:

- making sure employees receive feedback and coaching
- confirming there are plans in place to evaluate employee performance
- verifying that development plans are targeted to the needs of the organization.

The PMBOK® Guide says Project Human Resource Management includes the processes that organize, manage, and lead the project team.

To track human resource management you must:

- Plan human resource management.
- Acquire a project team.
- Develop a project team.
- Manage a project team.

The human resources forms in this section include:

1. Training Human Resource Management Plan
2. Training Coaching/Mentoring Log
3. Training Project Staffing Requirements
4. Training Individual Development Plan
5. Training Individual Performance Evaluation
6. Training Job Snapshot Task
7. Training Position Description
8. Training Presentation: Presenter Profile
9. Training Professional Skills Checklist
10. Training RACI Matrix
11. Training Resource Pool
12. Training Resource Requirements
13. Training Responsibility Assignment Matrix
14. Training Rewards and Recognition
15. Training Team Biography
16. Training Team Building
17. Training Team Directory
18. Training Team Agreement

Training Human Resource Management Plan

Project Title: _____

Project Description:

Planning human resource management will involve:

Acquiring the project team will involve:

Developing the project team will involve:

Managing the project team will involve:

Notes:

Prepared by: _____ Date: _____

Contact Information: _____

Project Manager: _____ Project Due Date: _____

Training Coaching/Mentoring Log

Project Title: _____

Project Description:

Process ☐ Coaching ☐ Mentoring ☐ Other: _____

History

Date	Name	Assigned to	Outcome and Next Steps	Time Invested

Notes:

Prepared by: _____ Date: _____

Contact Information: _____

Project Manager: _____ Project Due Date: _____

Training Project
Staffing Requirements

Project Title: _____

Project Description:

Responsibilities

Name	Role	Description	Start Date	End Date

Process, Procedure, Policy, or Practice	Employee or Contractor	Assigned Date	Due Date	Completed (Y/N)

Notes:

Prepared by: _____ Date: _____

Contact Information: _____

Project Manager: _____ Project Due Date: _____

Training Individual Development Plan

Project Title: _____

Project Description:

☐   Employee   ☐   Contractor

Name: _____   Phone: _____

Email: _____

Development Record

Assigned Date	Completion Date	Development Requirement	Program Description	Level of Importance: High (H), Medium (M), or Low (L)	Required (R), Suggested (S), or Optional (O)

Related to obtaining certification: ☐ Yes ☐ No

Related to certification maintenance: ☐ Yes ☐ No

Related to career path (new position or promotion): ☐ Yes ☐ No

Details:

Program Overview:

Notes:

Prepared by: _____ Date: _____

Contact Information: _____

Project Manager: _____ Project Due Date: _____

Training Individual Performance Evaluation

Project Title: _____

Project Description:

☐ Employee   ☐ Contractor

Name: _____ Phone: _____

Email: _____

Performance Evaluation

Project Management Focus Area	Supervisor Review Expectations: Failed to Meet (F), Met (M), or Exceeded (E)	Peer Review Expectations: Failed to Meet (F), Met (M), or Exceeded (E)	Key Stakeholders Expectations: Failed to Meet (F), Met (M), or Exceeded (E)
Communication			
Cost			
Human Resource			

Project Management Focus Area	Supervisor Review Expectations: Failed to Meet (F), Met (M), or Exceeded (E)	Peer Review Expectations: Failed to Meet (F), Met (M), or Exceeded (E)	Key Stakeholders Expectations: Failed to Meet (F), Met (M), or Exceeded (E)
Integration			
Procurement			
Quality			
Risk			
Scope			
Stakeholder			
Time			
Initiating			

Project Management Focus Area	Supervisor Review Expectations: Failed to Meet (F), Met (M), or Exceeded (E)	Peer Review Expectations: Failed to Meet (F), Met (M), or Exceeded (E)	Key Stakeholders Expectations: Failed to Meet (F), Met (M), or Exceeded (E)
Planning			
Executing			
Monitoring and Controlling			
Closing			

Recommendations for improving performance:

Notes:

Prepared by: _____ Date: _____

Contact Information: _____

Project Manager: _____ Project Due Date: _____

Training Job Snapshot Task

Project Title: _____

Project Description:

Technology

MS Office		

Abilities

Travel on plane		

Knowledge

Project management		

Notes:

Prepared by: _____   Date: _____

Contact Information: _____

Project Manager: _____   Project Due Date: _____

Training Position Description

Project Title: _____

Project Description:

Position Title: _____

Career Ladder Level/Grade (HR Input): _____

Position Purpose:

- The incumbent is a _____

Organizational Relationships:

- Reports to _____

- Liaises with _____

Resources are Managed:

- Direct reports are _____

- Dotted line reports are _____

Primary Duties:

The primary job function will be determined for the candidate based on his or her experience, skills, and overall business needs, but is expected to encompass the following:

- _____

- _____

- _____

- _____

- _____

Training and Education Preferred:

- _____
- _____
- _____

Prior Experience Preferred:

- _____
- _____
- _____

Technical Competencies:

- _____
- _____
- _____

Behavioral Competencies:

- _____
- _____
- _____

The candidate's style appears to be:

Notes:

Prepared by: _____ Date: _____

Contact Information: _____

Project Manager: _____ Project Due Date: _____

Training Presentation: Presenter Profile

Project Title: _____

Project Description:

Learning Objectives:

1. _____
2. _____
3. _____

Presenter Profile

☐ Existing Vendor	☐ New Vendor	Company Name _____
Primary Contact: _____		Secondary Contact: _____
Phone: _____		Phone: _____
Email: _____		Email: _____
Mailing Address: _____ _____ _____ _____		

Presenter Biography: _____

_____

_____

Presenter Level 1 Evaluation History (if Available):

Rating (1st, 2nd, or 3rd): _____

Ranking (Poor, Fair, or Good): _____

Grading (A, B, C, D, or F): _____

Audio/Visual Equipment Requirements for Presentation:

- ☐ Laptop Projector   ☐ Whiteboard   ☐ Easel
- ☐ Easel Paper   ☐ Name Tents
- ☐ Special content created by author (for example, books): _____

Technology Platform for Presentation:

- ☐ On-Site Training (local)   ☐ Teleconference (no video)   ☐ Skype
- ☐ WebEx   ☐ Microsoft NetMeeting
- ☐ Microsoft LiveMeeting   ☐ GoToMeeting
- ☐ Other: _____

Training Room Design Configuration:

- ☐ Classroom   ☐ Clustered tables   ☐ Standing
- ☐ U-shaped   ☐ Other

Presenter Presentation Status:

- ☐ Presenter CV on file.
- ☐ Presenter résumé on file.
- ☐ Presenter references on file.
- ☐ Presenter presentation has been received.
- ☐ Presenter presentation has been reviewed/approved.

Notes:

Prepared by: _____ Date: _____

Contact Information: _____

Project Manager: _____ Project Due Date: _____

Training Professional Skills Checklist

Project Title: _____

Project Description:

Vendor Capabilities (check all that apply):

☐ Project Management

☐ Instructional Design

☐ Curriculum Development

☐ Animation Creation

☐ Image Editing

☐ Learning Management Systems Administration

☐ Job Function Curriculum Determination

☐ Software Programming, specify _____

☐ E-Learning Development

☐ Storyboarding

☐ Narration

☐ Digital Music Creation

☐ Narration Scripting

☐ Assembling Training Manuals

☐ Creating Job Aids

☐ Laminating Documents

☐ In-Person, Instructor-Led Training

☐ Web-Based, Instructor-Led Training

☐ Graphics Creation

☐ Technical Writing

☐ Information Mapping

☐ Process Mapping

☐ Logic Modeling

☐ Flow Charting

☐ Value Stream Mapping

☐ Creating Illustrations

☐ Cartooning

☐ Compliance Auditing

☐ Training Evaluation

☐ Needs Assessment

☐ Coaching

☐ Mentoring

☐ Data Archiving

☐ Training Evaluation

☐ Facilitating Lessons Learned

☐ Facilitating Brainstorming Sessions

☐ Teambuilding Exercises

☐ Creating Rewards and Recognition Programs

☐ Cloud-Based Document Back-Up

☐ Other: _____

Training-Related Software Proficiency (check all that apply):

☐ Adobe Premiere

☐ Adobe Audition

☐ Adobe Photoshop

☐ Adobe Illustrator

☐ Adobe Presenter

☐ Adobe Flash

☐ Adobe Acrobat

☐ Adobe Dreamweaver

☐ Adobe Captivate

☐ Adobe Director

☐ Adobe Authorware

☐ Adobe PageMaker

☐ Adobe FrameMaker

☐ Adobe RoboHelp

☐ Adobe After Effects

☐ Adobe InDesign

☐ Adobe Analytics

☐ Other Adobe:_____

☐ Articulate Storyline

☐ Articulate Presenter

☐ Articulate Quiz Maker

☐ Articulate Engage

☐ Articulate Online

☐ Lectora Snap

☐ Lectora E-Learning Suite

☐ SumTotal LMS

☐ Plateau LMS

☐ MS Word

☐ MS PowerPoint

☐ MS Excel

☐ MS Outlook

☐ MS SharePoint

☐ MS Visio

☐ MS Access

☐ MS Publisher

☐ Pedagogue

☐ Snag It Screen Capture

☐ Camtasia

☐ Smith Micro Poser

☐ Smart Draw

☐ Other: _____

Training Logistics:

☐ Onboarding New Hires

☐ Off-Boarding Resources

☐ New Hire and Transfer Orientation

☐ Scheduling Facilities

☐ Facilitating Workshops

☐ Coordinating Conferences

☐ Facilitating Meetings

☐ Setting Up Paper-Based Training Files

☐ Entering Data Into the Training Learning Management System

☐ Running Training Reports

☐ Reviewing Training Reports

Training-Related Certifications (list all that apply)

Name	Abbreviation	Type	Association

Notes:

Prepared by: _____ Date: _____

Contact Information: _____

Project Manager: _____ Project Due Date: _____

Training RACI Matrix

Project Title: _____

Project Description:

Training Deliverables Assigned

Deliverable	Instructional Designer	Curriculum Developer	Training Administrator	Trainer

Notes:

Prepared by: _____   Date: _____

Contact Information: _____

Project Manager: _____   Project Due Date: _____

Training Resource Pool

Project Title: _____

Project Description:

Weekly Schedule

Name or Initials	Availability							
	Week 1	Week 2	Week 3	Week 4	Week 5	Week 6	Week 7	Week 8

Name or Initials	Availability							
	Week 1		Week 2		Week 3		Week 4	
	8–12	1–5	8–12	1–5	8–12	1–5	8–12	1–5

Name or Initials	Week 5		Week 6		Week 7		Week 8	
	8–12	1–5	8–12	1–5	8–12	1–5	8–12	1–5

Notes:

Prepared by: _____ Date: _____

Contact Information: _____

Project Manager: _____ Project Due Date: _____

Training Resource Requirements

Project Title: _____

Project Description:

Capabilities Match Up

Skill Set Needed	Assigned Name From Resource Pool	Availability							
		Week 1		Week 2		Week 3		Week 4	
		8–12	1–5	8–12	1–5	8–12	1–5	8–12	1–5

Skill Set Needed	Assigned Name From Resource Pool	Availability							
		Week 1		Week 2		Week 3		Week 4	
		8–12	1–5	8–12	1–5	8–12	1–5	8–12	1–5

Notes:

Prepared by: _____ Date: _____

Contact Information: _____

Project Manager: _____ Project Due Date: _____

Training Responsibility Assignment Matrix

Project Title: _____

Project Description:

Alignment

Date Assigned	Name	Start Date	Title	Responsibility	Email	Phone

Notes:

Prepared by: _____ Date: _____

Contact Information: _____

Project Manager: _____ Project Due Date: _____

Training Rewards and Recognition

Project Title: _____

Project Description:

Reward Recipients:

☐ Individual ☐ Team ☐ Large Group ☐ Company

☐ Contractor

Recognition:

☐ Certificate ☐ Letter ☐ Money ☐ Gift Card

☐ Other: _____

Event

Date	Participant Name	Activity Description

Notes:

Prepared by: _____ Date: _____

Contact Information: _____

Project Manager: _____ Project Due Date: _____

Training Team Biography

Project Title: _____

Project Description:

Work Experience:

Education/Professional Certifications:

Noteworthy Achievements:

Professional Associations or Affiliations:

Personal Interests:

Notes:

Prepared by: _____   Date: _____

Contact Information: _____

Project Manager: _____   Project Due Date: _____

Training Team Building

Project Title: _____

Project Description:

Event Options:

☐ Outward Bound	☐ Ropes Course	☐ GPS Scavenger Hunt
☐ Bowling	☐ Paintball	☐ Laser Tag
☐ Roller Coaster Park	☐ Softball	☐ Breakfast
☐ Luncheon	☐ Dinner	☐ Other:_____

Record of Events

Date	Participant Name	Activity Description

Notes:

Prepared by: _____ Date: _____

Contact Information: _____

Project Manager: _____ Project Due Date: _____

Training Team Directory

Project Title: _____

Project Description:

Contact Information

Date Joined	Name	Role	Phone	Email

Notes:

Prepared by: _____ Date: _____

Contact Information: _____

Project Manager: _____ Project Due Date: _____

Training Team Agreement

Project Title: _____

Project Description:

Comments

	Team Member	Value Statement
1		
2		
3		
4		
5		
6		

	Team Member	Value Statement
7		
8		
9		
10		

Notes:

Prepared by: _____ Date: _____

Contact Information: _____

Project Manager: _____ Project Due Date: _____

INTEGRATING PROJECTS

Project Integration involves identifying, defining, combining, unifying, and coordinating activities across Initiating, Planning, Executing, Monitoring and Controlling, and Closing (the five project management Process Groups).

Team members must work closely to keep the project well integrated across the activities and functional areas of the organization. This requires attention to detail and focus on all aspects of the project. Experience is an important factor to project oversight. Empowering the right people to do good work is an important aspect of leadership.

Lessons learned can be conducted at the end to determine:

- the return on investment of a training program by tracking expenditures forms
- results and level of satisfaction with a course through an evaluation form
- accountability—who did what by tracking with forms.

Lessons learned can be conducted formatively to address:

- process improvement, by looking at how to better coordinate instructor schedules through forms
- change management, by documenting change requests with forms
- business continuity, by looking at backing-up electronic training documentation with forms.

The Training Issues Log captures concerns for the overall training project and documents those concerns for training-related events. Examples include:

- availability of facilities
- requirements for developing content in more than the native language
- enabling additional training platforms or connectivity to support business continuity requirements
- emerging requirements for blended learning solutions, when additional ways of delivering the same content in different ways becomes highly desirable.

The training business case, research, and supporting documentation are used during the creation of the project charter and serve as the foundation for the project and ongoing operations. For example, a key stakeholder initiates a great idea for a new training program, but does not know how to justify the $100,000 it will cost to fund the project. He works in conjunction with a project manager with experience in T&D who reviews case studies on similar projects and determines the return on investment for the organization. This business case is presented to senior management who become the sponsors for the project.

Forms help the integration process in many ways by:

- ensuring there is a valid business case for embarking upon a training project
- verifying that all the work of the project is coordinated
- confirming that the necessary processes are in place to manage change.

The PMBOK® Guide says Project Integration Management includes the processes required to identify, define, combine, unify, and coordinate the various processes and project management activities within the project management Process Groups.

To manage training project integration you must:

- Develop a project charter.

- Develop a project management plan.
- Direct and manage project work.
- Monitor and control project work.
- Perform integrated change control.
- Close the project or phase.

The integration forms in this section include:

- Training Integration Management Plan
- Training Change Request
- Training Formal Acceptance of Deliverable
- Training Issues Log
- Training Project Charter

Training Integration Management Plan

Project Title: _____

Project Description:

Developing the project charter will involve:

Developing the project management plan will involve:

Directing and managing project work will involve:

Monitoring and controlling project work will involve:

Performing integrated change control will involve:

Closing the project or phase will involve:

Notes:

Prepared by: _____ Date: _____

Contact Information: _____

Project Manager: _____ Project Due Date: _____

Training Change Request

Project Title: _____

Project Description:

Description of change:

Reason for change:

Affect if change request is approved or not approved:

Change control number or configuration management details:

Decision:

    ☐ Approved   ☐ Denied   ☐ Pending   ☐ Other _____

Notes:

Approvers

Name	Title	Signature	Date (mm/dd/yyyy)

Notes:

Prepared by: _____ Date: _____

Contact Information: _____

Project Manager: _____ Project Due Date: _____

Training Formal Acceptance
of Deliverable

Project Title: _____

Project Description:

Description of deliverable(s):

Agreed upon acceptance criteria:

Approval Signatures

Date	Name	Title	Deliverable

Notes:

Prepared by: _____ Date: _____

Contact Information: _____

Project Manager: _____ Project Due Date: _____

Training Issues Log

Project Title: _____

Project Description:

Issues Tracker

Date	Concern	Status (R, Y, or G)	Impact on Objectives (H, M, or L)	Person Responsible	Due Date for Resolution

Notes:

Prepared by: _____ Date: _____

Contact Information: _____

Project Manager: _____ Project Due Date: _____

Training Project Charter

Project Title: _____

Project Overview:

Project Purpose:

Project Description:

Project Objectives:

Project Goals:

Integrating Projects

Project Assumptions:

Project Constraints:

Project Critical Success Factors:

Notes:

Prepared by: _____ Date: _____

Contact Information: _____

Project Manager: _____ Project Due Date: _____

MANAGING PROCUREMENT

Managing procurement involves acquiring products, services, or results from outside the performing organization (project team). Even in the most sophisticated training organizations, there are services that require expertise from a vendor, such as the implementation of a large-scale learning management system.

The training team, in conjunction with the purchasing department, is involved in the procurement process, which involves negotiating with and managing:

- vendors
- consultants
- suppliers
- contractors
- other third parties.

Vendor management can be very challenging due to complexities that arise involving:

- drafting legal contracts
- working with temporary resource firms who serve as referral agencies for contractors
- dealing with employment and sometimes labor union problems
- training contactors on company policies and procedures
- ensuring the work of contractors meets quality expectations

- managing contractor schedules
- protecting intellectual property so that it does not end up in the hands of its competitors
- managing requirement changes
- contractors accessing, collaborating, and sharing files.

Training project managers are challenged with:

- locating high quality contractors who are able to work on short projects
- retaining high quality contractors on a cost effective basis
- justifying the use of external contractors if internal training resources exist
- integrating external contractors with internal company employees
- requiring contractors to perform at the level and commitment of internal team members.

Forms help the procurement process in many ways, including:

- ensuring correspondence can be tracked
- formalizing agreements through contracts
- addressing any gaps not covered in contracts with appropriate documentation.

The PMBOK® Guide says Project Procurement Management includes the processes necessary to purchase or acquire products, services, or results needed from outside the project team. The organization can be either the buyer or seller of the products, services, or results of a project.

To manage procurement you must:

- Plan procurement management.
- Conduct procurements.
- Control procurements.
- Close procurements.

The procurement forms in this section include:

1. Training Procurement Management Plan
2. Training Quality Agreement
3. Training Request for Information
4. Training Request for Proposal
5. Training Service Level Agreement
6. Training Services Contractor Agreement
7. Training Statement of Work
8. Training Vendor Capabilities Summary
9. Training Vendor Performance Evaluation
10. Training Vendor Qualification

Training Procurement Management Plan

Project Title: _____

Project Description:

Planning procurement management will involve:

Conducting procurements will involve:

Controlling procurements will involve:

Closing procurements will involve:

Notes:

Prepared by: _____ Date: _____

Contact Information: _____

Project Manager: _____ Project Due Date: _____

Training Quality Agreement

Project Title: _____

Project Description:

Summary of the quality agreement:

Parties to the Agreement

Company	Name	Signature
Customer		
Vendor		
Other Third Parties		

Items in Quality Agreement

Item	Description
Scope	
Duration	

Corrective and Preventative Actions

Item	Description

Record Retention Policies

Item	Description

Performance Reporting

Item	Description

Auditing Procedures

Item	Description

Complaint Resolution and Escalation Process

Item	Description

Glossary

Item	Description

Notes:

Prepared by: _____ Date: _____

Contact Information: _____

Project Manager: _____ Project Due Date: _____

Training Request for Information

Project Title: _____

Project Description:

Summary statement of work:

Request Type:

☐ Capabilities Brochure (printed or electronic) ☐ Demonstration

☐ Simulation (on-the-job training) ☐ Presentation (PowerPoint or webinar)

☐ Documentation (procedure, diagram) ☐ Work Sample

☐ Other: _____

Requirements

Details Regarding Request(s)	Due Date

Stakeholder Review

People Involved in Reviewing Information	Feedback

Notes:

Prepared by: _____ Date: _____

Contact Information: _____

Project Manager: _____ Project Due Date: _____

Training Request for Proposal

Project Title: _____

Project Description:

Summary statement of work:

RFP Type:

- ☐ Open Solicitation
- ☐ Closed Bid (contacted potential suppliers)
- ☐ Reverse (contacted by vendor)

If a reverse RFP (vendor initiated), are comparable bids sought from this proposal?

- ☐ Yes
- ☐ No

If a reverse RFP (vendor initiated), is it being provided under terms of non-disclosure?

- ☐ Yes
- ☐ No

Requirements

Details Regarding Deliverable(s)	Start Date	Due Date	Projected Cost

Contract Type:

☐ Hourly _____ per hour   ☐ Fixed Price _____

☐ Additional Charges _____

Notes:

Prepared by: _____   Date: _____

Contact Information: _____

Project Manager: _____ Project Due Date: _____

Training Service Level Agreement

Project Title: _____

Project Description:

General Overview:

Period of Coverage:

Service Description:

Roles and Responsibilities

Name	Function	Contact Information

Service Request Process:

Hours of Operation:

Prioritizing Requests:

Escalation:

Rates and Charges:

Performance Reporting:

Glossary:

References:

Approvers

Date	Name	Contact Information

Notes:

Prepared by: _____ Date: _____

Contact Information: _____

Project Manager: _____ Project Due Date: _____

Training Services
Contractor Agreement

Project Title: _____

Project Description:

Contractor Contact Information:

Project Start Date: _____

Project End Date: _____

Deliverables:

Consultant's Background:

Consultant's Roles and Responsibilities:

Confidentiality Agreement:

Indemnity and Applicable Law:

Independent Contractor Status:

Payment Terms:

Approvals

Date	Name	Deliverable

Notes:

Prepared by: _____ Date: _____

Contact Information: _____

Project Manager: _____ Project Due Date: _____

Training Statement of Work

Project Title: _____

Project Description:

Customer Contact Information:

Project Start Date: _____

Project End Date: _____

Deliverables:

Payment Terms:

Contract Type:

Approvals

Date	Name	Deliverable

Notes:

Prepared by: _____ Date: _____

Contact Information: _____

Project Manager: _____ Project Due Date: _____

Training Vendor Capabilities Summary

Project Title: _____

Project Description:

Summary of Vendor Capabilities:

Samples Provided:

Links to Examples:

Notes:

Prepared by: _____ Date: _____

Contact Information: _____

Project Manager: _____ Project Due Date: _____

Training Vendor
Performance Evaluation

Project Title: _____

Project Description:

Vendor Profile

☐ **Existing Vendor**	☐ **New Vendor**	☐ **Continue With Vendor**	☐ **Discontinue With Vendor**
Primary Contact: _____ Secondary Contact: _____ Phone: _____ Phone: _____ Email: _____ Email: _____ Mailing Address: _____ _____ _____ _____			

☐   Rating (1st, 2nd, or 3rd)

☐   Ranking (Poor, Fair, or Good)

☐   Grading (A, B, C, D, or F)

Feedback on Vendor Received

Date	Deliverable	Stakeholder	Comments

Notes:

Prepared by: _____ Date: _____

Contact Information: _____

Project Manager: _____ Project Due Date: _____

Training Vendor Qualification

Project Title: _____

Project Description:

Vendor Profile

☐ **Existing Vendor**	☐ **New Vendor**	☐ **References Checked**	☐ **Vendor Paperwork Completed**
Primary Contact: _____ Secondary Contact: _____ Phone: _____ Phone: _____ Email: _____ Email: _____ Mailing Address: _____ _____ _____ _____			

Entity Designation:

☐   Corporation   ☐   Partnership   ☐   Sole Proprietorship

☐   Other, specify _____

Details:

Product or Service Capabilities:

Identified Product or Service Limitations:

History of Working With This Vendor:

☐ Rating (1st, 2nd, or 3rd)   ☐ Ranking (Poor, Fair, or Good)
☐ Grading (A, B, C, D, or F)

Financial Information

Taxpayer Identification Number: _____ SSN#: _____

Bank Account Information: _____

Bonded/Insured: ☐ No   ☐ Yes $_____

Required for Project: ☐ No   ☐ Yes

Other: _____

References

Company	Product/Service Provided	Contact

Notes:

Prepared by: _____ Date: _____

Contact Information: _____

Project Manager: _____ Project Due Date: _____

MANAGING QUALITY

Managing quality involves defining quality policies, goals, and roles. This is managed to ensure that the end product satisfies the needs of the project.

When quality is not clearly defined, the expectations of a training project can be unclear. What represents quality to the CEO of the organization might be different than what quality represents to the learner. For example, the CEO may be anticipating impressive looking participant materials, whereas the participants need simple, easy-to-modify job aids.

The quality of training deliverables produced is ultimately the responsibility of the training project manager. Here are some things the training team should consider with respect to producing quality training deliverables:

- Quality must be clearly defined at the beginning of the project.

- The definition of quality should be in writing and agreed to by stakeholders. It should address what makes the project acceptable.

- Everyone on the project team should be committed to quality.

- The depth and breadth of training materials often becomes better the longer you have to work on them or the number of resources that are available to work on them.

- Visual appeal and other sensory elements—for example, graphics, sound, colors, animation, music, games, pop-quizzes, and video—have a tendency to make users believe the quality of training materials is higher.

- Beta testing to the appropriate target audience to gain acceptance before a roll-out is one of the best ways to determine the current quality of a deliverable.

- Creative and critical thinking skills are important in both instructional design and curriculum development efforts. Having people with different personalities and opinions work on projects can result in good outcomes.

- Some organizations adhere to Kaizen principles or have continuous improvement philosophies. These may result in training projects with new procedures or quality-related deliverables.

Forms in the area of quality can be valuable for many reasons, including:

- ensuring that training is compliant

- maximizing the return-on-investment for specific training initiatives

- auditing training to ensure that compliance meets regulatory requirements.

The PMBOK® Guide says Project Quality Management includes the processes and activities that determine quality policies, objectives, and responsibilities so that the project will satisfy the needs for which it was undertaken.

To manage quality you must:

- Plan quality management.

- Perform quality assurance.

- Control quality.

This section includes the following forms:

1. Training Quality Management Plan
2. Archived Training Project Documents
3. Training Audit Checklist
4. Training Resource Requirements
5. Kirkpatrick's Four Levels of Evaluation Template
6. Training Good Business Practices
7. Training Performance Gap Analysis

8. Training Performance Metrics
9. Periodic Training Review
10. ROI/ROQ Evaluation

Training Quality Management Plan

Project Title: _____

Project Description:

Planning quality management will involve:

Performing quality assurance will involve:

Controlling quality will involve:

Notes:

Prepared by: _____ Date: _____

Contact Information: _____

Project Manager: _____ Project Due Date: _____

Archived Training Project Documents

Project Title: _____

Project Description:

Document Repository

Last Revision Date	Archive Date	Document Title	Version	Location	Submitted by	Storage Method

Last Revision Date	Archive Date	Document Title	Version	Location	Submitted by	Storage Method

Notes:

Prepared by: _____ Date: _____

Contact Information: _____

Project Manager: _____ Project Due Date: _____

Training Audit Checklist

Project Title: _____

Project Description:

Typical Documents Requested During an Audit

Item Is Accessible: Compliance Assurance	Yes	No	Comment
Organization Charts (Include Upper Management)			
Address and Telephone Listing of Management			
Site Overview Diagram			
Street Address of All Buildings			
Size of Facility			
Hours of Operation			

Item Is Accessible: Compliance Assurance	Yes	No	Comment
Number of Employees			
Site Operations: Number of Shifts			
Union Employees			
Non-Union Employees			
List of Products Produced at the Site			
List of Services Offered at the Site			
List of Product Complaints			
History of Service Complaints			
List of Change Controls			

Item Is Accessible: Compliance Assurance	Yes	No	Comment
General Policies			
Company Handbook			
SOP Index			
Change Control Procedures			
Training Histories			
Training Job Function Curriculum			
Training Assessment (Test Results)			
Training Procedures			
Annual Compliance Training Programs			

Item Is Accessible: Compliance Assurance	Yes	No	Comment
Job Descriptions of Training Team Members			
Locations of Training Files (Paper and Electronic)			
Training Remediation Activities and Investigations			

Notes:

Prepared by: _____ Date: _____

Contact Information: _____

Project Manager: _____ Project Due Date: _____

Training Resource Requirements

Project Title: _____

Project Description:

Background, Introduction, Overview, Purpose, Objectives, and Goals:

1. Does the course provide the learner with a statement of its direction?

   - Does it break down the initial parts into individual sections?
   - Does the information flow from beginning to end and include summaries?

2. Will the course motivate the user to learn?

   - Does it establish the content as a source of knowledge or information that is useful to them?
   - Does it engage the learner in activities (such as knowledge checks or exercises)?

3. Have the objectives been clearly defined, stated in terms of:

   - What type of learner should be taking the course?
   - What should learners be able to do after they have completed the course?
   - Is there alignment between the scope (objectives) and amount of instructional content?

Design Considerations:

1. Has the audience been defined?

   - Primary (main)
   - Secondary (others)

2. Has prerequisite knowledge been defined?

   - Did participants complete the pre-work?
   - Does the pre-work tie into main course?

3. Is the material free from bias?

   - Cultural and place of residence (race or ethnicity)
   - Gender and sexual preference
   - Age

4. Does the course incorporate multimedia?
   - Graphics
   - Video
   - Audio
   - Animation
   - Simulations

Course Mechanics:

1. Is the information clearly presented?
   - Language
   - Concepts
   - Terms and definitions
2. Is the course segmented properly?
   - Modules
   - Length of content within
3. Is the courseware user friendly?
   - Is online help enabled?
   - Is technical support available?
4. Is the screen layout optimal?
   - Appropriate use of white space
   - Text size is clear and easily readable
5. Is the material grammatically correct?
   - No spelling errors
   - No grammar mistakes
6. Are terms defined?
   - Is a glossary provided?
   - Are acronyms and abbreviations understood?

Navigation:

1. Can the course be controlled by the user?
   - Can the users determine how far they have gone in the course at any given time?
   - Can the users exit the course at any time?
   - Can the users return to the same place from which they exited (is there bookmarking)?

- Can they go backward and forward, without skipping content, in the course?
- Are navigation icons and other elements (such as text-based menus) used consistently in the course?

2. Can navigation control be restricted?
   - Can copying content be stopped?
   - Can ALT-tabbing to other applications be stopped?
   - Can multiple windows be opened if a procedure needs to be referenced?

Notes:

Prepared by: _____ Date: _____

Contact Information: _____

Project Manager: _____ Project Due Date: _____

Kirkpatrick's Four Levels of Evaluation Template

Project Title: _____

Project Description:

Level 1 Evaluation Program Summary:

Level 2 Evaluation Program Summary:

Level 3 Evaluation Program Summary:

Level 4 Evaluation Program Summary:

Notes:

Prepared by: _____ Date: _____

Contact Information: _____

Project Manager: _____ Project Due Date: _____

Training Good Business Practices

Project Title: _____

Project Description:

Title: _____ Number: _____

Version: _____ Effective Date: _____

Purpose:

Scope:

Role Definition

Title	Responsibilities

Recommendations:

Revision History

Summary of Changes	Rationale

Approvals

Date	Name	Title

Notes:

Prepared by: _____ Date: _____

Contact Information: _____

Project Manager: _____ Project Due Date: _____

Training Performance Gap Analysis

Project Title: _____

Project Description:

Human Performance Technology Approach

Performance Need	Treatment Need (1)	Treatment Need (2)	Training Requirement	Supporting Solution(s)
Alternative Methods				

Employee or Contractor	Name	Phone	Email

Notes:

Prepared by: _____ Date: _____

Contact Information: _____

Project Manager: _____ Project Due Date: _____

Training Performance Metrics

Project Title: _____

Project Description:

Report Date: _____

Department: _____

Location: _____

Performance Metrics

Trainee Name	Satisfaction With Training Program (1-5)	Test Score(s) Percentage (%)	30-Day Post Training (1-5)	90-Day Post Training Impact (1-5)

Cost (1-5)	Time (1-5)	Scope (1-5)	Quality (1-5)	Risk (1-5)	Resources (1-5)

Notes:

Prepared by: _____ Date: _____

Contact Information: _____

Project Manager: _____ Project Due Date: _____

Periodic Training Review

Project Title: _____

Project Description:

Review of System, Program, Process, Policy, or Procedure

Description	Review Date	Due Date	Meets Quality Standards Yes (Y) or No (N)	Resolution

Are there any compliance issues?

☐ No   ☐ Yes, specify:

Are there any investigations?

    ☐   No   ☐   Yes, specify:

Are there any deviations from procedures?

    ☐   No   ☐   Yes, specify:

Notes:

Prepared by: _____ Date: _____

Contact Information: _____

Project Manager: _____ Project Due Date: _____

ROI/ROQ Evaluation

Project Title: _____

Project Description:

Analysis:

- Return on Investment (ROI) = (Financial Project Benefits ÷ Program Costs) x 100

$$ROI = \left(\frac{FIN}{PRO}\right) \times 100$$

- Return on Quality (ROQ) = (Quality-Related Project Benefits ÷ Program Investments) x 100

$$ROQ = \left(\frac{QRP}{PI}\right) \times 100$$

Program Investments	Training Project Cost	Financial or Quality-Related Benefit	Description of Benefit	Impact of Benefit	Value of Benefit
ROI looks at program costs, as well as one-time and recurring expenditures that can be monetized.					
ROQ looks at things from a qualitative and approximated quantitative perspective. Program investments attempt to consider financial expenditures and other items of monetary value.					

Factors associated with estimating training project cost:

Project Management Formulas

Name	Term	Interpretation
PV (AKA) BCWS	Planned Value (AKA) *Budgeted Cost of Work Scheduled*	What is the estimated value of the work planned to be done? The 50/50 rule states when beginning a task, charge 50 percent of the PV to its account (the other 50 percent upon completion).
EV (AKA) BCWP	Earned Value *Budgeted Cost of Work Performed*	What is the estimated value of the work actually accomplished?
AC (AKA) ACWP	Actual Cost *Actual Cost of Work Performed*	What is the actual cost incurred?
BAC	(AKA) Budget at Completion	How much did we budget for the total job?

Name	Formula	Interpretation
Cost Variance (CV)	EV – AC	Negative is over budget, positive is under budget.
Schedule Variance (SV)	EV – PV	Negative is behind schedule, positive is ahead of schedule.
Cost Performance Index (CPI)	EV/AC	We are getting $____ out of every $1. Cumulative CPI refers to the sum of all individual EVs divided by the sum of all individual ACs. It is used to forecast project cost at completion.
Schedule Performance Index (SPI)	EV/PV	We are [only] progressing at ___ percent of the rate originally planned. A value equal to or greater than one indicates a favorable condition and a value less than one indicates an unfavorable condition.

Estimate at Completion (EAC) (AKA) Latest Revised Estimate (LRE) **NOTE:** There are four ways to calculate EAC. The first formula on the right is most often used.	1. BAC/CPI 2. AC + ETC 3. AC+BAC-EV 4. AC+(BAC-EV) CPI	As of now, how much do we expect the total project to cost? $_____. • Used if no variances from BAC have occurred or will continue at same rate of spending. • Actual plus a new estimate for remaining work. Used when original estimate was fundamentally flawed. (In other words used when past assumptions are incorrect.) • Actual to date plus remaining budget. Used when current variances are thought to be atypical of the future. (In other words used when variances are not typical.) • Actual to date plus remaining budget modified by performance. Used when current variances are thought to be typical of the future. (When variances are expected to remain the same.)
Estimate to Completion (ETC)	EAC – AC	How much more will the project cost?
Variance at Completion (VAC)	BAC – EAC	How much over budget will we be at the end of the project?

Notes:

Prepared by: _____   Date: _____

Contact Information: _____

Project Manager: _____   Project Due Date: _____

MANAGING RISK

Managing risk involves conducting, planning, identifying, analyzing, responding to, and controlling project uncertainties (both positive and negative).

Effectively managing risk in training projects is the responsibility of the training project manager. Potential risks to look for in training projects and ongoing operations include:

- not recognizing or identifying stakeholders
- unannounced external training audits by regulatory authorities
- incorrect or missing training assignments
- outdated or obsolete training
- lack of blended training approaches
- inaccessibility to training content
- misperception of the importance of training
- minimal or no continuous improvement

Risk management can be categorized into knowledge areas:

- Communications
- Cost
- Human Resources
- Integration
- Procurement
- Quality
- Scope

- Stakeholder

- Time.

Risks can also be viewed in terms of the life of the project, by process groups:

- Initiation

- Planning

- Executing

- Monitoring and Controlling

- Closing.

The PMBOK® Guide says Project Risk Management includes the processes of conducting risk management planning, identification, analysis, response planning, and controlling risk on a project. The objectives of project risk management are to increase the likelihood and impact of positive events, and decrease the likelihood and impact of negative events in the project.

To manage risk for your training project you must:

- Plan risk management.

- Identify risks.

- Perform qualitative risk analysis.

- Perform quantitative risk analysis.

- Plan risk responses.

- Control risk.

The following forms are included in this section:

1. Training Risk Management Plan

2. Business Continuity Plan

3. Training Risk Management Scales

4. Training Risk Mitigation Strategies

5. Training Risk Probability/Impact Matrix

6. Training Risk Register

7. Training SWOT Analysis

Training Risk Management Plan

Project Title: _____

Project Description:

Planning risk management will involve:

Identifying risks will involve:

Performing qualitative risk analysis will involve:

Performing quantitative risk analysis will involve:

Planning risk responses will involve:

Controlling risks will involve:

Notes:

Prepared by: _____ Date: _____

Contact Information: _____

Project Manager: _____ Project Due Date: _____

Business Continuity Plan

Project Title: _____

Project Description:

Business Continuity Procedures

Title	Version	Effective Date	Description

Business Continuity Focus:

- ☐ Succession Planning   ☐ Change Management
- ☐ Disaster Recovery   ☐ Contingency
- ☐ Other: _____

Business Continuity Issues:

- ☐ Lost Records   ☐ Misplaced Records
- ☐ Stolen Records   ☐ Falsified Records/Records in Question of Validity
- ☐ LMS Performance Issues   ☐ LMS Temporary Outage
- ☐ LMS Anticipated Long-Term Outage

    ☐ LMS Administrator Currently Unavailable

    ☐ LMS Vendor Currently Unavailable

    ☐ Trainer Currently Unavailable

    ☐ Training Management Currently Unavailable

    ☐ Trained Employee Currently Unavailable

    ☐ Other, specify: _____

Proposed Solutions:

Notes:

Prepared by: _____ Date: _____

Contact Information: _____

Project Manager: _____ Project Due Date: _____

Training Risk Management Scales

Project Title: _____

Project Description:

Scales

Event	Severity	Probability	Detectability	Effect
	Dangerously High			
	Extremely High			
	Very High			
	High			
	Moderately High			
	Medium			
	Low			
	Very Low			
	Extremely Low			
	Almost Non-Existent			

Notes:

Prepared by: _____   Date: _____

Contact Information: _____

Project Manager: _____   Project Due Date: _____

Training Risk Mitigation Strategies

Project Title: _____

Project Description:

Capabilities Match Up

Identified (Potential) Risk Factors	Risk Mitigation Techniques

Notes:

Prepared by: _____   Date: _____

Contact Information: _____

Project Manager: _____   Project Due Date: _____

Training Risk Probability/ Impact Matrix

Project Title: _____

Project Description:

PxI Rating: High (H), Medium (M), and Low (L)

Risk Event	Probability	Impact on Cost	Impact on Time	Impact on Scope	Overall Impact (Averages)	Overall Risk Rating (Probability x Overall Impact)
Unavailability of training materials						
Unexpected weather						

Summary of Results:

Notes:

PxI Rating: Numeric Values (Below .4 = low, .4-.6 = med, above .7 = high)

Risk Event	Probability	Impact on Quality	Impact on Resources	Impact on Stakeholders	Overall Impact (Averages)	Overall Risk Rating (Probability x Overall Impact)

Probability Almost Certain	0.90	0.09	0.27	0.45	0.63	0.83
	0.70	0.07	0.21	0.35	0.49	0.63
	0.50	0.05	0.15	0.25	0.35	0.45
	0.30	0.03	0.09	0.15	0.21	0.27
Very Unlikely	0.10	0.01	0.03	0.05	0.07	0.09
		0.10	0.30	0.50	0.70	0.90

Impact on Project Objective

Probability Almost Certain	Mod	Mod	High	High	High
	Mod	Mod	Mod	High	High
	Low	Mod	Mod	Mod	High
	Low	Low	Mod	Mod	Mod
Very Unlikely	Low	Low	Low	Mod	Mod
	Very Low	Low	Mod	High	Very High

Impact on Project Objective

Notes:

Prepared by: _____   Date: _____

Contact Information: _____

Project Manager: _____   Project Due Date: _____

Training Risk Register

Project Title: _____

Project Description:

Register

Priority	Identified Potential Risk	Probability (H, M, or L) or Numeric	Impact (H, M, or L) or Numeric	Overall Risk Rating (H, M, or L) or Numeric	Status (R, Y, or G)	Person Assigned

Notes:

Prepared by: _____   Date: _____

Contact Information: _____

Project Manager: _____   Project Due Date: _____

Training SWOT Analysis

Project Title: _____

Project Description:

Strengths:

Weaknesses:

Opportunities:

Threats:

Notes:

Prepared by: _____ Date: _____

Contact Information: _____

Project Manager: _____ Project Due Date: _____

MANAGING SCOPE

Managing scope involves verifying that the specified work has been successfully completed and only the work required becomes part of the project.

Scope creep occurs when the objectives of the training program change without proper approvals. Costs increase, development schedules become longer, resources become strained, and risk increases. Therefore, measures must be put into place to eliminate scope creep. Possible measures include:

- Use training forms to document project progress.
- Understand the stakeholder's wants and needs by defining requirements clearly at the beginning of the project.
- Institute a formal change control process.
- Request a management reserve or contingency reserve to deal with possible cost over-runs.
- Involve key stakeholders in status meetings.
- Publish meeting minutes.
- Assign action items to key stakeholders to keep them involved in the project.
- Remain transparent about the impact that changes in scope have on the project.
- Calculate the amount of time needed to complete scope change.
- Keep a record of scope changes and the affect they have on the project.
- Remain flexible and anticipate changes to the project, especially if working in an Agile environment.

- When reporting use green-yellow-red indicators so that progress is clearly depicted.

- Utilizing network diagrams, such as the Diagramming Method (PDM), when appropriate to show any variances to plan.

- Consider using Gantt charts to show milestones reached and the benefits of minimizing scope creep.

- Shift available resources to fill gaps that may be caused by scope creep.

- Have a clear understanding of needs in the project.

- Learn to say no to unnecessary or unreasonable scope requests.

- If working with vendors, review service level agreements for additional costs due to scope change.

- Do not over-emphasize scope changes that are small and that can be done quickly.

- Do not appear unresponsive or inflexible to addressing approved scope changes.

- Thank project team members who effectively address scope creep.

Forms help manage scope by:

- defining the work of the project in terms of deliverables

- ensuring that only the work required is part of the project and completed

- requiring additional requests follow the approved change control process.

The PMBOK® Guide says Project Scope Management includes the processes to ensure the project includes all the work required—and only the work required—to complete the project successfully. Managing the project scope is primarily concerned with defining and controlling what is and is not included in the project.

To manage scope you must:

- Plan scope management.

- Collect requirements.

- Define scope.

- Create a work breakdown structure.
- Validate scope.
- Control scope.

The following forms are included in this section:

1. Training Scope Management Plan
2. Training Benchmarking
3. Training Blended Learning Approaches
4. Training Content Media Reference
5. Training Instructional Design—Curriculum Development
6. Training Professional Delivery Checklist
7. Training Request Form
8. Training Scope Statement
9. Smart Training Objectives
10. Training Variance Analysis

Training Scope Management Plan

Project Title: _____

Project Description:

Planning scope management will involve:

Collecting requirements will involve:

Defining scope will involve:

Creating WBS will involve:

Validating scope will involve:

Controlling scope will involve:

Notes:

Prepared by: _____ Date: _____

Contact Information: _____

Project Manager: _____ Project Due Date: _____

Training Benchmarking

Project Title: _____

Project Description:

Comparison

Company	Deliverable	Scope	Time to Develop	Required Resources	Cost to Develop	Quality Rating 1 (Low) 5 (High)	Details

Notes:

Prepared by: _____ Date: _____

Contact Information: _____

Project Manager: _____ Project Due Date: _____

Training Blended Learning Approaches

Project Title: _____

Project Description:

Alternate Delivery Options

Method	Pros	Cons	Factors to Consider
Instructor-led (in-person)			
Instructor-led (remote)			
Job aid			
Reviewing a procedure			
Group activity			
Workshop			

Method	Pros	Cons	Factors to Consider
Observation			

Notes:

Prepared by: _____ Date: _____

Contact Information: _____

Project Manager: _____ Project Due Date: _____

Training Content Media Reference

Project Title: _____

Project Description:

History

Date	Content/Medium	Created by	Description

Notes:

Prepared by: _____ Date: _____

Contact Information: _____

Project Manager: _____ Project Due Date: _____

Training Instructional Design—Curriculum Development

Project Title: _____

Project Description:

Stage 1. Needs Assessment:

Stage 2. Concept:

Stage 3. Design:

Stage 4. Make/Buy Determination

Develop (Make)		Acquire (Buy)	
Pros	Cons	Pros	Cons

Stage 5. Go/No-Go Decision:

Stage 6. Development:

Stage 7. Alpha Test:

Stage 8. Pilot:

Stage 9. Deployment:

Stage 10. Evaluation:

Notes:

Prepared by: _____ Date: _____

Contact Information: _____

Project Manager: _____ Project Due Date: _____

Training Professional Delivery Checklist

Project Title: _____

Project Description:

Skill #1. Validate course material:

☐ Review training materials and identify areas where revisions are required.

☐ Confirm that the appropriate instructional design methods have been followed.

☐ Check to make sure curriculum development processes have been followed in the creation of training material.

☐ Make minor adjustments to training materials.

Skill #2. Analyze your audience:

☐ Review target audience for completeness.

☐ Sort participants as necessary into categories; for example, on-site versus virtual.

☐ Identify other potential stakeholders who might be included in future training.

☐ Record attendance of participants.

Skill #3. Assure optimal operation of the training environment:

☐ Confirm logistical arrangements, agenda, start and stop times, and similar.

☐ Ensure the appropriateness of the training environment of the instructional site, gather training materials, make sure equipment is working, adjust heating and cooling, check and address cleanliness, and arrange refreshments, equipment, and furniture.

☐ Establish points of connection for any virtual attendees.

☐ Publish the schedule so that it can be viewed by attendees.

Skill #4. Establish instructor credibility:

☐ Introduce the instructor and supporting subject matter experts.

☐ Present biography to establish presence.

☐ Model professional behavior.

☐ Demonstrate flexibility in response to participants' interests.

Skill #5. Adapt to the learning styles:

☐ Adhere to adult learning principles.

☐ Encourage active participation.

☐ Align the presentation strategies to meet program objectives.

☐ Remain flexible to adjust activities as necessary.

Skill #6. Use instructional methods appropriately:

☐ Balance the use of handouts.

☐ Keep in mind the 6x6 rule for presentations (six words per line and six bullets per slide).

☐ Integrate multimedia components to make the training dynamic.

☐ Implement blended training as necessary (combination of training approaches).

Skill #7. Maintain effective communication skills:

☐ Use appropriate nonverbal communication.

☐ Be conscious of tone (paralinguistics).

☐ Maintain appropriate tone of voice.

☐ Utilize common language and avoid slang.

Skill #8. Demonstrate dynamic presentation skills:

☐ Use gestures, silence, movement, posture, space, and props effectively.

☐ Illustrate with anecdotes, stories, analogies, and humor effectively.

☐ Diagram, map, and chart to engage the audience.

☐ Have participants use index cards or sticky notes to get them involved.

Skill #9. Facilitate through questioning and obtaining feedback:

☐ Create a parking lot for questions.

☐ Respond appropriately to questions.

☐ Use active listening techniques.

☐ Repeat, rephrase, or restructure questions.

Skill #10. Provide reinforcement:

☐ Reinforce desirable behaviors.

☐ Politely correct unfavorable behaviors.

☐ Encourage those who don't participate.

☐ Balance feedback coming from different participants.

Skill #11. Evaluate training:

☐ Consider qualitative and quantitative approaches.

☐ Administer assessments (Level 1, 2, 3, or 4).

☐ Review assessments and arrive at conclusions.

☐ Report on assessments.

Notes:

Prepared by: _____ Date: _____

Contact Information: _____

Project Manager: _____ Project Due Date: _____

Training Request Form

Project Title: _____

Project Description:

Requestor Contact Information

Name:		Telephone:	
Title:		Department:	
Email Address:		Cost Center:	
Implementation Date:		Meeting Date:	
Details:			

Current situation:

Describe the training requirement:

Describe the performance issues:

Describe the behaviors to be addressed:

Describe the expected impact the training will have:

Describe the primary target audience (titles, responsibilities, departments, and number of people):

Describe the secondary audience (for example, contracts and vendors):

Describe the desired training environment (instructor-led, self-study, or e-learning):

Describe the desired length of the training:

Describe any special needs (for example, provisions for wheelchairs, or the hearing impaired):

Notes:

Prepared by: _____   Date: _____

Contact Information: _____

Project Manager: _____   Project Due Date: _____

Training Scope Statement

Project Title: _____

Project Description:

Business Case:

Supporting Documents

Type	Source	Details

Objectives:

Description:

Deliverables:

Requirements:

Out of Scope:

Acceptance Criteria:

Project Team Members:

Identified Risks:

Scheduled Milestones:

Cost Estimates:

Other Specifications:

Approval Requirements:

Notes:

Prepared by: _____   Date: _____

Contact Information: _____

Project Manager: _____   Project Due Date: _____

Smart Training Objectives

Project Title: _____

Project Description:

The purpose of writing objectives is to guide performance. Well-written objectives provide clear expectations against which we can measure our success. When objectives are aligned with the organization's goals, we can establish a clear link between performance and compensation and ensure that the performance we get is worth paying for.

SMART objectives are:

- Specific: why, who, which, and what

- Measurable: time, amount, quantity, quality

- Achievable: can be accomplished based upon who we are and/or what we have access to

- Realistic: make good business sense

- Time-based: when it will be completed—how long in terms of duration

Smart Object Statement: _____

Notes:

Prepared by: _____ Date: _____

Contact Information: _____

Project Manager: _____ Project Due Date: _____

Training Variance Analysis

Project Title: _____

Project Description:

Type of Variance (select all that apply)

Knowledge Area:

☐ Communications   ☐ Cost   ☐ Human Resource

☐ Integration   ☐ Procurement   ☐ Quality

☐ Risk   ☐ Scope   ☐ Stakeholder

☐ Time

Process Group:

☐ Initiating   ☐ Planning   ☐ Executing

☐ Monitoring and Controlling   ☐ Closing

Description of Variance:

Impact of Variance:

Solution:

Corrective Action	Preventative Action (Future)

Notes:

Prepared by: _____   Date: _____

Contact Information: _____

Project Manager: _____   Project Due Date: _____

MANAGING STAKEHOLDERS

Managing stakeholders involves identifying the individuals or entities that could affect or be affected by the project, evaluating stakeholder expectations and their influence on the project, and developing strategies for involving stakeholders in project decisions and work.

Working with various stakeholders on training projects can be very challenging because:

- Stakeholders have different personalities.

- Some stakeholders have agendas that are different from the project objectives.

- Stakeholders may be busy and unavailable.

- Stakeholders have different levels of interest that vary over time, based upon circumstances and involvement.

- Organizational politics and culture affect stakeholder attitudes and perspectives.

- Stakeholders may be located at a different location or a different time zone.

- Stakeholders may be from different cultures.

- Stakeholders may even be external to the organization—the community could be a stakeholder. Having to narrow a focus when identifying stakeholders is a potential risk in projects.

Some of the keys to improving stakeholder relations include:

- Follow good principles of working with stakeholders as outlined by well-respected authors such as Stephen Covey (*Seven Habits of Highly Effective People*) and Dale Carnegie (*How to Win Friends and Influence People*).

- Have a system for identifying stakeholders and working with them consistently based upon factors such as stakeholder power and influence.

- Build relationships with stakeholders by getting to know them on a personal basis.

- Be transparent with stakeholders by letting them get to know you on a professional basis.

- Periodically touch base with stakeholders by following the agreed upon communications plan.

- Understand and implement the individual stakeholder's preferred communication method.

Things to be mindful of when dealing with stakeholders:

- Avoid any gossip, rumors, or negative conversations.

- Be on time for any meeting, formal or informal.

- Remain positive when circumstances become challenging.

- Classify conversations as confidential (not to be repeated), to be shared selectively after receiving permission, and open to share without permission (general knowledge).

- Stakeholders speak with other stakeholders and will influence their perception of you.

- A genuine compliment or sincere thank you goes a long way in developing relationships.

- Some people may have patterns of being more responsive at certain times of the day or week.

Forms can be essential in working with key contacts by:

- identifying levels of power and influence on a project

- organizing people into logical groups to help formalize communication

- determining what information that should be given to specific people or groups.

The PMBOK® Guide says project stakeholder management includes the processes required to identify the people, groups, or organizations that could affect or be affected by the project; analyze stakeholder expectations and their impact on the project, and to develop appropriate management strategies for effectively engaging stakeholders in project decisions and execution.

To manage stakeholders you must:

- Identify stakeholders.

- Plan stakeholder management.

- Manage stakeholder engagement.

- Control stakeholder engagement.

The stakeholder forms in this section include:

1. Training Stakeholder Management Plan

2. Training Brainstorming Worksheet

3. Training Daily Sign-in Tracking Sheet

4. Training Job Function Curriculum

5. Training Media Release

6. Training Stakeholder Analysis

7. Training Stakeholder Contact History

8. Training Stakeholder Register

9. Training Stakeholder Satisfaction Survey

10. Training Weekly Sign-in Tracking Sheet

Training Stakeholder Management Plan

Project Title: _____

Project Description:

Identifying stakeholders will involve:

Planning stakeholder management will involve:

Managing stakeholder engagement will involve:

Controlling stakeholder engagement will involve:

Notes:

Prepared by: _____ Date: _____

Contact Information: _____

Project Manager: _____ Project Due Date: _____

Training Brainstorming Worksheet

Project Title: _____

Project Description:

Discussion Topics

Under Consideration	Possible Solutions

Under Consideration	Possible Solutions

Notes:

Prepared by: _____ Date: _____

Contact Information: _____

Project Manager: _____ Project Due Date: _____

Training Daily Sign-in Tracking Sheet

Project Title: _____

Project Description:

Daily Schedule

Date	Name	Organization	Phone	Email

Start Time: _____

End Time: _____

Course Duration: _____

Notes:

Prepared by: _____ Date: _____

Contact Information: _____

Project Manager: _____ Project Due Date: _____

Training Job Function Curriculum

Project Title: _____

Project Description:

LMS Database:

Name Title ID #: _____

☐ Employee   ☐ Contractor

Supervisor: _____

Department: _____

Work Location: _____

Course Title	Procedure	Version	Training Method	Date Assigned	Date Due	Date Completed	Pass / Fail % Score	Mandatory (M) or Optional (O)

Notes:

Prepared by: _____ Date: _____

Contact Information: _____

Project Manager: _____ Project Due Date: _____

Training Media Release

Project Title: _____

Project Description:

In consideration for the use of my photograph, voice, or image, I _____(name) do hereby give _____ (name of company), its successors, assigns, licensees, and legal representative the irrevocable right to use my name (or any fictional name), picture, likeness, portrait, photograph, or sound in all forms and media (which specifically includes Internet use and any and all electronic media that now exists or may exist in the future), and in all manners, techniques, or methods, with whatever content, graphics, sound, or images _____ (name of company) chooses as its sole discretion, worldwide and without restriction as to frequency or duration of use, for any commercial or non-commercial purpose, including, but not limited to, advertising, trade, packaging, point-of-sale materials, training and development, lessons learned, and/or any other lawful purpose. I waive any right to inspect or approve the finished versions, including written copy that may be created in connection therewith. I waive the right to any intellectual knowledge, ways of knowing, information, or data associated with this communication. I hereby release _____ (name of company), its successors, assigns, licensees, and legal representatives from any liability concerning any blurring, distortion, or alteration, whether intentional or otherwise, that may occur or be produced in the taking or in the use of picture, voice, likeness, portrait, or photograph. I have read this release and am fully familiar and in agreement with its contents. I certify that I am 18 years of age or older, have the full right to contract in my own name with respect to the matters stated above, and have no conflicting advertising or promotional commitments that would make me unable to enter into and fully grant the rights specified by this release. This consent and release shall be binding upon my heirs, next of kin, and personal representatives. _____ (name of company), its successors, and assigns shall be the absolute owner of any and all materials (and all rights therein, include the copyright) produced pursuant to this release.

Date: _____

Name: _____ Signature: _____

Parent or legal guardian: _____

Signature: _____

Witness or notary (print): _____

Signature: _____

———————————— Consent, if applicable ————————————

Check here if applicable:

☐ I am the parent or guardian of the minor named above and have the legal authority to execute the above release. I approve the foregoing and waive any rights in the premises.

Training Stakeholder Analysis

Project Title: _____

Project Description:

Place descriptors or code names (not real names).

High		
Influence		
Low	**Concern**	**High**

- Upper Right: Invest the most time and ensure they are getting exactly what they want.

- Upper Left: Make sure they are happy and will remain an advocate for you.

- Lower Right: Make sure they have the information they need and are not worried.

- Lower Left: Let them be, unless they can be moved to the upper left and become an advocate.

Notes:

Prepared by: _____ Date: _____

Contact Information: _____

Project Manager: _____ Project Due Date: _____

Training Stakeholder Contact History

Project Title: _____

Project Description:

Alignment

Stakeholder Name	Project Team Member Assigned	Issue	Communication Method	Date

Notes:

Prepared by: _____ Date: _____

Contact Information: _____

Project Manager: _____ Project Due Date: _____

Training Stakeholder Register

Project Title: _____

Project Description:

Profile

Stakeholder Name	Title	Role in Project	Preferred Communication Method	Frequency

Stakeholder Name	Personality Style	Amount of Influence	Level of Interest	Contact Information

Stakeholder Name	Project Team Member Assigned	Date Assigned	Secondary Contact Project Team Member	Details

Stakeholder Name	Stakeholder's Supervisor	Stakeholder's Supervisor Contact Information	Reason to Contact Substitute or Boss	Alternate if Stakeholder is Unavailable

Notes:

Prepared by: _____ Date: _____

Contact Information: _____

Project Manager: _____ Project Due Date: _____

Training Stakeholder Satisfaction Survey

Project Title: _____

Project Description:

Feedback on Project

Stakeholder Satisfaction Survey	Strongly Disagree	Disagree	Somewhat Disagree	Somewhat Agree	Agree	Strongly Agree
Survey Metrics: Respondents Indicated						

Actions Based on Survey Results:

Notes:

Prepared by: _____ Date: _____

Contact Information: _____

Project Manager: _____ Project Due Date: _____

Training Weekly
Sign-in Tracking Sheet

Project Title: _____

Project Description:

Weekly Schedule (By Half Day):

Start Time: _____End Time: _____

Details:

Notes:

Prepared by: _____ Date: _____

Contact Information: _____

Project Manager: _____ Project Due Date: _____

Name or Initials	Mon. AM	Mon. PM	Tues. AM	Tues. PM	Wed. AM	Wed. PM	Thurs. AM	Thurs. PM	Fri. AM	Fri. PM	Sat. AM	Sat. PM	Sun. AM	Sun. PM

MANAGING TIME

Managing time involves planning, sequencing, estimating, and controlling the project schedule.

The training project manager is accountable for how he uses his time, as well as how other team members schedule their activities. Here are some considerations for managing time on training-related projects and ongoing operations:

- The average office worker (project team member) may have 75 percent productive time in an eight-hour workday. Focus effort on helping office workers increase both the perceived amount of productive time (50-75 percent of an eight-hour workday), as well as becoming more industrious above the estimated level.

- The training project manager needs to understand how people use their time and acknowledge competing priorities. If activities are sequenced in a different order, it could help people become more productive.

- Identify the type of team members. For example, are they people who like to be constantly busy because it makes their day go faster and it increases their sense of value and contribution to the team? Or do they get overwhelmed by a high quantity of work all at once?

- Principles of time management need to address what can be done differently to streamline work. Eliminating duplicate efforts is an essential part of streamlining work.

- Lean environments support the philosophy of doing more with less.

- Tracking time is a necessary process. By putting everything on a schedule, the amount of wasted time can be uncovered.

- Saving time on training-related projects and operations involves learning how to work smarter, focusing on the work that needs to be done.

Forms help the time management process in many ways by:

- ensuring that there is a sequence to the order in which training deliverables are created

- supporting the return on time investment for complex projects

- validating the expenses incurred on projects by looking at how long things take.

The PMBOK® Guide says project time management includes the processes required to manage the timely completion of the project.

To manage time efficiently you must:

- Plan schedule management.

- Define activities.

- Sequence activities.

- Estimate activity resources.

- Estimate activity durations.

- Develop the schedule.

- Control the schedule.

This section includes the following forms:

1. Training Project Time Management Plan

2. Training Gantt Chart

3. Training Milestone Chart

4. Training Network Diagram

5. Training Time Tracker

6. Training Time-Based Learning Journal

7. Training Timesheet

8. Training Trends Report

9. Training Work Breakdown Structure

TRAINING PROJECT TIME MANAGEMENT PLAN

Project Title: _____

Project Description:

Planning schedule management will involve:

Defining schedule activities will involve:

Sequencing schedule activities will involve:

Estimating activity resources will involve:

Estimating activity durations will involve:

Developing the schedule will involve:

Controlling the schedule will involve:

Notes:

Prepared by: _____ Date: _____

Contact Information: _____

Project Manager: _____ Project Due Date: _____

Training Gantt Chart

Project Title: _____

Project Description:

Q1 2014 (One-month Gantt Chart based on a Monday–Friday schedule)

Task Name	(Date Beginning Project)																			
	M	T	W	T	F	M	T	W	T	F	M	T	W	T	F	M	T	W	T	F
Needs Assessment																				
Survey																				
Focus Group																				
Observation																				
Instructional Design																				
Meeting SMEs																				
Storyboarding																				
Scripting																				
Prototyping																				
Curriculum Development																				
Case Studies																				
Scenarios																				
Quizzes																				
Instructor-Led Delivery																				
On-site																				
Webinar																				
On Call by Phone																				

Notes:

Prepared by: _____ Date: _____

Contact Information: _____

Project Manager: _____ Project Due Date: _____

Training Milestone Chart

Project Title: _____

Project Description:

Q1 2014 (One-month chart based upon a Monday–Friday schedule)

Task Name	(Date Beginning Project)																			
	M	T	W	T	F	M	T	W	T	F	M	T	W	T	F	M	T	W	T	F
Needs Assessment																				
Person Responsible																				
Instructional Design																				
Person Responsible																				
Curriculum Development																				
Person Responsible																				
Instructor-Led Delivery																				
Person Responsible																				

Notes:

Prepared by: _____ Date: _____

Contact Information: _____

Project Manager: _____ Project Due Date: _____

Training Network Diagram

Project Title: _____

Project Description:

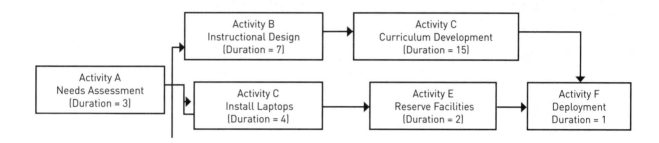

Training Work Breakdown Structure

Activity	Duration	Description	Assigned to	Date
A				
B				
C				
D				
E				
F				

Notes:

Prepared by: _____ Date: _____

Contact Information: _____

Project Manager: _____ Project Due Date: _____

Training Time Tracker

Project Title: _____

Project Description:

Activity Record

Date	Event	Start Time	End Time	Details
	Certification Test			

Notes:

Prepared by: _____   Date: _____

Contact Information: _____

Project Manager: _____   Project Due Date: _____

Training Time-Based Learning Journal

Project Title: _____

Project Description:

Key Learning Record

Date	Time	Location	Event	People Involved	Take away

Notes:

Prepared by: _____ Date: _____

Contact Information: _____

Project Manager: _____ Project Due Date: _____

Training Timesheet

Project Title: _____

Project Description:

Name:				Week Ending:					
Emp #/SSN/Tax ID:				Dept. #:					
Employee Title:				Employee Type:					
Employee Status:				Employee Class:					
Client Name:				Supervisor:					
Project ID:			**Hours Worked**						
Cost Center:		**Sun**	**Mon**	**Tue**	**Wed**	**Thu**	**Fri**	**Sat**	**Total**
Description	**Receipt**								
	Total								

Date	Employee/Contractor Signature
Date	Approval Signature
Notes	

Managing Time

Prepared by: _____ Date: _____

Contact Information: _____

Project Manager: _____ Project Due Date: _____

Training Trends Report

Project Title: _____

Project Description:

Training Method

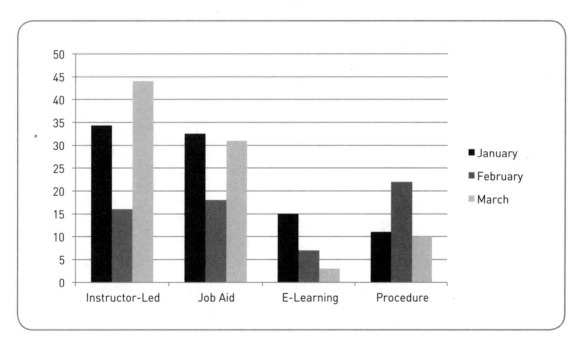

Number of employees who participated in each training program:

Training Method					
Month	Instructor-Led	Job Aid	E-Learning	Procedure	Notes
January	34				
February	16				
March	44				

Notes:

Prepared by: _____ Date: _____

Contact Information: _____

Project Manager: _____ Project Due Date: _____

Training Work Breakdown Structure

Project Title: _____

Project Description:

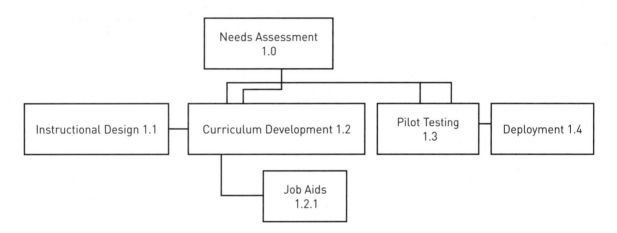

Outline View
- 1.0 – Needs Assessment
- 1.1 – Instructional Design
- 1.2 – Curriculum Development
- 1.2.1 – Job Aids
- 1.3 – Pilot Testing
- 1.4 – Deployment

WBS No.	Task	Description	Details
1.0	Needs Assessment		
1.1	Instructional Design		
1.2	Curriculum Development		
1.2.1	Job Aids		
1.3	Pilot Testing		
1.4	Deployment		

Notes:

Prepared by: _____ Date: _____

Contact Information: _____

Project Manager: _____ Project Due Date: _____

APPENDIX I
ABBREVIATIONS

Activity on Arrow	AOA
Activity on Node	AON
Analyze, Design, Develop, Implement, Evaluate	ADDIE
Arrow Diagramming Method	ADM
Association for Talent Development	ATD
Aviation Industry Computer-Based Training Committee	AICC
Certified Performance Technologist	CPT
Certified Professional in Learning and Performance	CPLP
Computer-Based Training	CBT
Define, Measure, Analyze, Improve, Control	DMAIC
Earned Value Analysis	EVA
Human Performance Technology	HPT
Instructor-Led Training	ILT
International Society of Performance Improvement	ISPI
Invitation for Bid	IFB
Learning and Development	L&D
Learning Management System	LMS
On-the-Job Training	OJT
Performance Improvement Plan	PIP
Precedence Diagramming Method	PDM
Program Evaluation Review Technique	PERT
Project Management Body of Knowledge	PMBOK®
Project Management Institute	PMI®
Project Management Professional	PMP®
Rapid Application Development	RAD
Request for Information	RFI
Request for Proposal	RFP
Return on Investment	ROI
Return on Quality	ROQ
Risk Breakdown Structure	RBS
Sharable Content Object Reference Model	SCORM
Skills, Knowledge, Ability	SKA
Statement of Work	SOW
Strengths, Weaknesses, Opportunities, Threats	SWOT

Appendix I

Time and Materials	T&M
Total Quality Management	TQM
Training and Development	T&D
What's in It for Me	WIIFM
Work Breakdown Structure	WBS

APPENDIX II
TERM DEFINITIONS

Agile Environment

The Agile environment is dynamic in that development is done in sprints and requires project team members to quickly respond to changes in requirements. Software programming is an example of an Agile environment. Agile is lean and quick by comparison to other development cycles, such as Spiral or Waterfall.

Arrow Diagramming Method (ADM)

ADM is a diagramming technique in which activities are represented by arrows. The tail of the arrow represents the beginning of the activity, and the head indicates the finish. Activities are connected at nodes to represent the sequence in which they are expected to be performed. In a training project, ADM could be used to show the relationship between instructional design and curriculum development.

Certified Training Professional

An individual who has demonstrated competency in training as required by a professional association or certifying body, such as the American Society for Training & Development, which offers the Certified Professional in Learning and Performance certification, or the International Society of Performance Improvement, which offers the Certified Performance Technologist certification. Some certified training professionals pursue a project management certification, such as the Project Management Professional from the Project Management Institute.

Change Control Board

This is a group of individuals who support revisions or special requests to a project. They meet periodically to approve change controls.

Change Management

Change management involves tactical and strategic techniques to support a smoother transition to organizational and cultural environments. Training in the form of orientation is critical to the success of change management. Training professionals may be called on to develop material; for example, posters, to help employees embrace culture change.

Cost of Quality

The costs incurred to ensure quality. This could include a variety of training interventions, such as re-reading procedures. It includes quality planning, quality control, quality assurance, and rework. The cost of quality can usually be justified by showing the cost of non-compliance. In other words, if training is not delivered, the impact it can have on the organization is determined.

Crashing

This is a duration compression technique that involves adding more resources to the project. Resources typically involve people, but may include systems, facilities, equipment, materials, and supplies. Crashing typically increases cost and risk. It could involve adding more resources to deliver more instructor-led training sessions in order to complete the training ahead of the original schedule.

Decomposition

Decomposition is breaking the work down into smaller, more manageable parts. A training professional will break down a training project into deliverables, such as procedure, job aid, participant manual, and instructor manual.

Duration Compression

Reducing the project schedule without reducing the project scope, examples include crashing and fast-tracking. Duration compression is not always possible and often requires an increase in project cost.

Earned Value Analysis

Determination of the investment made in a project is based upon factors such as cost, time, and scope. When earned value is calculated, it is important to determine how far the project deliverables have progressed as compared to the amount of resources (for example, money) invested. For example, a four-week training session is being conducted by an outside vendor who quoted $40,000 for one month to train staff on safety procedures. One week into the training it has been determined that 1/3 (33.3%) of the staff have been trained. It is estimated that the remaining staff can be trained within two weeks. The final cost could be $30,000 instead of $40,000 (depending upon contract terms and conditions). In this case, earned value would be positive because it is anticipated the training will be ahead of schedule (expected at one month) and below cost (expected at $40,000).

Effort

The number of labor units (work hours) required to complete an activity or other project element. This is generally expressed in hours, days, or weeks. For example the level of effort to produce a basic interactive one-hour e-learning course might be 80 development hours.

Engagement

Being engaged is involvement in a project; for example, when a training specialist facilitates a brainstorming session.

Fast Tracking

This is a duration compression technique that involves having resources multi-task. Resources typically are people, but may also include systems. For example, multi-tasking could involve having the trainer install training simulation software on more than one machine. This could reduce a schedule that was normally established in a serial sequence, with only one machine configured at a time.

Gantt Chart

A Gantt is a bar chart that contains schedule information. Activities are on the vertical axis and dates are on the horizontal bars. The training schedule of instructor-led delivery can be placed on a Gantt to show the duration.

Lessons Learned

Lessons learned is the process of gaining knowledge throughout the project to determine what went right, what went wrong, and what could have been done differently. The training professional can use this knowledge in a summative sense to address accountability or results, for an impact assessment. They may also do so in a formative sense to support process improvement, change management, or business continuity planning.

Lessonslearned.info

This is an informational website that provides resources to support project evaluation and lessons learned. Conducting lessons learned is a very important skill for training professionals who are involved in performance improvement initiatives. The supporting publication, *The Basics of Project Evaluation and Lessons Learned,* received the Cleland Award in 2012 from the Project Management Institute. The Cleland Award is given once per year recognizing the authors for significant contributions and for advancing project management knowledge, practices, procedures, concepts, or other advanced techniques that demonstrate the value of using project management.

Matrix Organization

A matrix represents an intersecting organization structure in which the project manager shares responsibility with the functional managers and assigns project work to others on the project team. The project manager may report to the VP of project management and be aligned to the marketing department. The project manager may be ultimately responsible for training programs and has a training specialist who completes job aids upon request.

Milestone
A milestone represents a recognized event in the project, usually the completion of a major deliverable, such as the approval of the training project plan.

Performance Reporting
Reporting performance involves collecting and disseminating performance information. This may include status reporting, progress measurement, and forecasting. For example, training statistics are reviewed in a call center environment.

Precedence Diagramming Method (PDM)
A network diagramming technique in which activities are represented by nodes. Activities are linked by precedence relationships to show the sequence in which the activities are to be performed. It is similar to ADM. For example, when the new laboratory technicians complete new hire orientation, they must go through a series of on-the-job training modules. These are diagrammed in a process flow chart, and each module must be completed in a sequence.

Probability and Impact Matrix
A common way to determine whether a risk is considered low, moderate, or high is by combining the two dimensions of a risk: its likelihood of occurring and impact if it occurs. This is commonly referred to as PxI. If detectability becomes a concern, the model then becomes PxIxD. Risk assessment is beneficial in cases in which whether to train or not to train has to be justified. Justification may be necessary due to cost, availability of trainers, or accessibility to trainees by taking them out of their normal job function.

Project Governance
The individual who is assigned the lead role on a project works in conjunction with the sponsor. There may also be a steering committee assigned to provide oversight for the project. The committee will work with the sponsor to provide governance. Some training projects are large-scale (global) and complex, involving engagement with different cultures. In these instances, governance can be of great value.

Project Management Information System (PMIS)
The software, hardware, communications equipment, data, and information stored on projects represent the PMIS. Microsoft Project is a common solution used by organizations and trainers for scheduling courses and facilities.

Quality Assurance (QA)
Quality assurance involves the defined and agreed upon activities that ensure a process or system conforms to requirements and meets or exceeds expectations. When a training program is installed on a computer server, QA will design the system to ensure that

the program runs successfully every time a user accesses it. This may involve creating procedures that deal with the implementation of the training program.

Responsibility Assignment Matrix (RAM)

The RAM is a document that is usually represented as a flow chart. It provides a graphical view that relates the project organization to the work to be performed, to ensure that each element of the project work is assigned to an accountable individual. The RAM could indicate who is responsible for performing the training needs assessment.

Root Cause Analysis

Root cause analysis involves determining the underlying or main causes of a problem. The fishbone diagram was developed in the late 1960s and has become a popular method for identifying factors that may contribute to a problem, such as a lack of on-the-job training.

Stakeholder

Stakeholders are individuals who have a vested interest in the project, or whose interests may be positively or negatively affected as a result of a project. Stakeholders may include trainees of a revised procedure.

Statement of Work (SOW)

An SOW is a written description of products, services, or results to be supplied under contract. For example, it could indicate the number of hours that the consultant will spend in a focus group getting opinions of specific key stakeholders.

SWOT Analysis

SWOT stands for Strengths, Weaknesses, Opportunities, and Threats. It is a method to conduct a risk assessment.

Three-Point Estimate

Optimistic, Pessimistic, and Most Likely outcomes are calculated to arrive at a realistic delivery date. For example, when the training administrator attempts to compute when the job-role curriculum will be input into the learning management system he states best case two weeks, worst case four weeks, and most likely three weeks.

Training Project Manager

Training professionals assigned the roles and responsibilities for training projects and in some cases ongoing operations. It is usually expected that they have project management skills (able to manage budgets, schedules, risk, vendors, quality, scope, and resources).

Voice of the Customer

Voice of the customer is a focused approach to determining requirements for a project. Trainers can work with subject matter experts to determine the actual needs versus wants.

Work Breakdown Structure (WBS)

A WBS is a logical, deliverable-oriented grouping of project work that conveys exactly what needs to be done. A WBS can be depicted graphically as a flow chart or as a list. The project level typically begins at level 1 (implementation of a learning management system) and each descending level represents the next level of detail of the project.

Work Package

A work package is a deliverable at the lowest level of the WBS. It may involve a media development effort that includes a PowerPoint presentation.

ABOUT THE AUTHOR

Willis H. Thomas, PhD, PMP, CPT has been involved in training and development, organizational effectiveness, and quality operations in the pharmaceutical, telecommunications, and information technology industries. As an employee, he has worked for large companies such as Xerox, Ameritech, Brinks, and Pfizer. As a consultant, he has worked for companies across many different industries around the globe, specifically in the areas of project management and evaluation.

He maintains a Project Management Professional (PMP) certification from the Project Management Institute (PMI®) and a Certified Performance Technologist (CPT) certification from the International Society of Performance Improvement (ISPI).

Willis is the author of a book published in November of 2011 entitled *The Basics of Project Evaluation* and Lessons Learned, by Productivity Press. His book was recognized as Best of the Best Publications by the Project Management Institute (PMI®) in October of 2012 and received the Cleland award at the PMI® Global Conference in Vancouver, Canada in 2012. He is also the author of *The Basics of Achieving Professional Certification: Enhancing Your Credentials*, published in November of 2013. He has been a guest speaker for numerous educational institutions and professional associations. He has authored a variety of articles on training and development, project management and evaluation in recognized journals, publications and websites. In the area of project management, he has taught many courses worldwide for the International Institute for Learning.

Willis holds a PhD in evaluation from Western Michigan University. The title of his dissertation was *A Metaevaluation of Lessons Learned Repositories: Evaluative Knowledge Management Practices in Project Management*. In line with his research, he has developed a comprehensive website on project management evaluation that focuses specifically on lessons learned at www.lessonslearned.info.

He has also served on the Dallas Chapter board of directors for ASTD and has been recognized as an outstanding volunteer.

HOW TO PURCHASE ATD PRESS PUBLICATIONS

ATD Press publications are available worldwide in print and electronic format.

To place an order, please visit our online store: www.td.org/books.

Our publications are also available at select online and brick-and-mortar retailers.

Outside the United States, English-language ATD Press titles may be purchased through the following distributors:

United Kingdom, Continental Europe, the Middle East, North Africa, Central Asia, and Latin America
Eurospan Group
Phone: 44.1767.604.972
Fax: 44.1767.601.640
Email: eurospan@turpin-distribution.com
Website: www.eurospanbookstore.com

Asia
Cengage Learning Asia Pte. Ltd.
Email: asia.info@cengage.com
Website: www.cengageasia.com

Nigeria
Paradise Bookshops
Phone: 08033075133
Email: paradisebookshops@gmail.com
Website: www.paradisebookshops.com

South Africa
Knowledge Resources
Phone: 27(11)880.8540
Fax: 27(11)880.8700/9829
Email: mail@knowres.co.za
Website: www.kr.co.za

For all other territories, customers may place their orders at the ATD online store: **www.td.org/books**.

101417 62220